EATING WELL

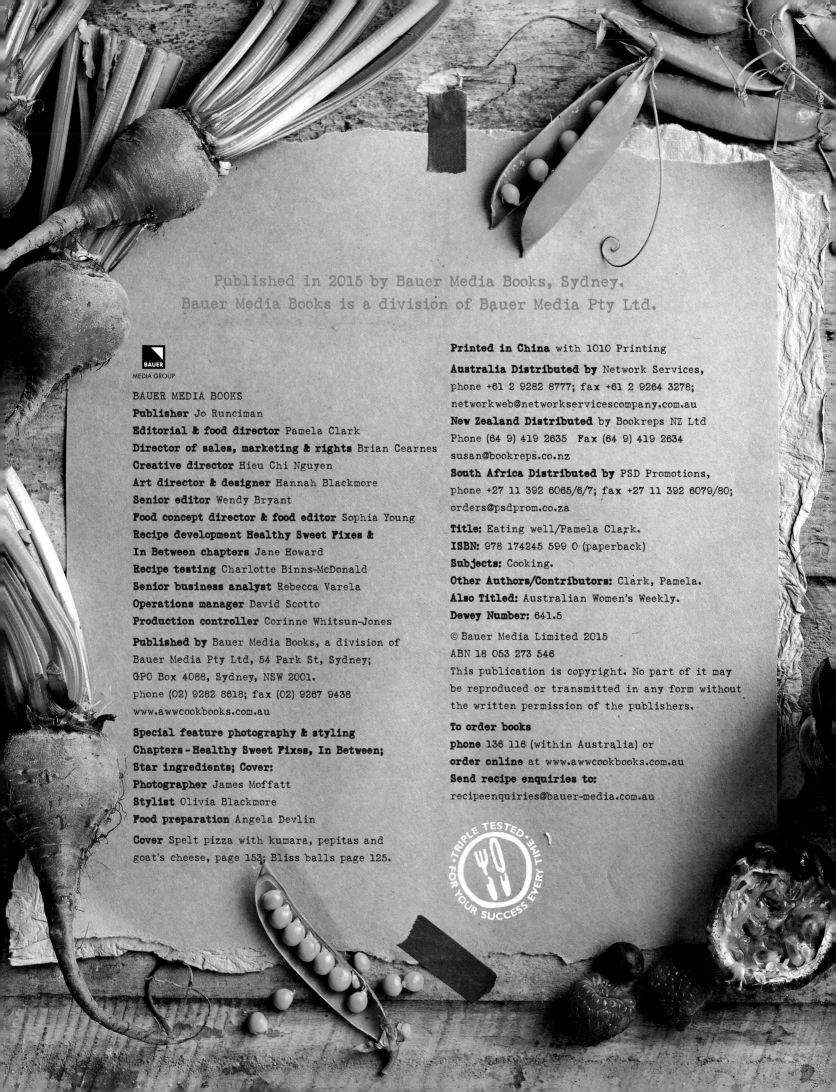

Published in 2015 by Bauer Media Books, Sydney.
Bauer Media Books is a division of Bauer Media Pty Ltd.

BAUER MEDIA BOOKS
Publisher Jo Runciman
Editorial & food director Pamela Clark
Director of sales, marketing & rights Brian Cearnes
Creative director Hieu Chi Nguyen
Art director & designer Hannah Blackmore
Senior editor Wendy Bryant
Food concept director & food editor Sophia Young
**Recipe development Healthy Sweet Fixes &
In Between chapters** Jane Howard
Recipe testing Charlotte Binns-McDonald
Senior business analyst Rebecca Varela
Operations manager David Scotto
Production controller Corinne Whitsun-Jones

Published by Bauer Media Books, a division of
Bauer Media Pty Ltd, 54 Park St, Sydney;
GPO Box 4088, Sydney, NSW 2001.
phone (02) 9282 8618; fax (02) 9267 9438
www.awwcookbooks.com.au

**Special feature photography & styling
Chapters – Healthy Sweet Fixes, In Between;
Star ingredients; Cover:**
Photographer James Moffatt
Stylist Olivia Blackmore
Food preparation Angela Devlin

Cover Spelt pizza with kumara, pepitas and
goat's cheese, page 153; Bliss balls page 125.

Printed in China with 1010 Printing
Australia Distributed by Network Services,
phone +61 2 9282 8777; fax +61 2 9264 3278;
networkweb@networkservicescompany.com.au
New Zealand Distributed by Bookreps NZ Ltd
Phone (64 9) 419 2635   Fax (64 9) 419 2634
susan@bookreps.co.nz
South Africa Distributed by PSD Promotions,
phone +27 11 392 6065/6/7; fax +27 11 392 6079/80;
orders@psdprom.co.za

Title: Eating well/Pamela Clark.
ISBN: 978 174245 599 0 (paperback)
Subjects: Cooking.
Other Authors/Contributors: Clark, Pamela.
Also Titled: Australian Women's Weekly.
Dewey Number: 641.5

To order books
phone 136 116 (within Australia) or
order online at www.awwcookbooks.com.au
Send recipe enquiries to:
recipeenquiries@bauer-media.com.au

· TRIPLE TESTED ·
FOR YOUR SUCCESS EVERY TIME!

THE AUSTRALIAN
Women's Weekly

EATING WELL

CONTENTS

EATING WELL

I've been a dietitian and nutritionist for over 15 years, and have had a passion for understanding how food and the way I eat affects my health and wellbeing since I was a teenager. When I started my career, most of the interest in the public domain and the media was all about weight control. Beyond that, not much thought was given. Fast-forward to today and we are awash with nutrition information - some theory, some opinion and some of it based on good science.

I'm delighted at this surge of interest. The recognition that what you choose to eat affects not just your weight, but the way you feel, how healthy you look, and how well your body and your brain works day to day, has dramatically changed the food landscape. Everyone is writing about nutrition from the most academically qualified to interested bloggers and everyone in between. I welcome this enthusiasm, but it does come with a problem. It's leaving many people utterly confused over what to eat.

With so many conflicting views, what on earth does 'eating well' mean?

The truth is it can mean many things. There is no such thing as The Perfect Diet. We are all different: some people will have allergies or intolerances to certain foods, while the same foods may be fabulous nutrient-rich choices for others. Some may have made an ethical choice not to eat animal foods, but vegetarian comes in many different forms; from a completely vegan diet to those who are willing to include eggs and dairy foods.

Many people living with diabetes are avidly aware their diet can affect their blood glucose control and, in the long term, their risk of other health complications.

And now there is also a growing number of people engaging in the paleo approach to eating - an attempt to replicate the diet of our hunter-gatherer ancestors.

All of these approaches can result in good or bad diets. So, whichever approach you choose, or have to follow, you must still give thought as to making the best food choices possible.

This is why I'm delighted to introduce this book, *Eating Well*, from the Australian Women's Weekly. This book is not about casting judgment on which approach is better - it's about giving you the tools, and the inspiration to make your dietary approach work for you, and to ensure it is as nutrient-rich, health promoting and, just as importantly, as delicious, as possible.

As a guide, you'll find each recipe indicates whether that recipe is suitable for your particular diet. The terms we use are as follows:

Diabetes-friendly indicates the recipes have been approved by Diabetes Australia as suitable for those living with diabetes.

Vegan indicates recipes that are suitable for vegan diets. These recipes contain only plant foods, and do not contain meat, seafood, eggs or dairy foods.

Vegetarian indicates recipes that contain no meat or seafood, but may contain dairy foods and/or eggs.

Lacto-vegetarian these recipes are suitable for vegetarians who are happy to eat dairy foods. They contain no meat, fish or eggs.

Ovo-vegetarian these recipes are suitable for vegetarians who are happy to eat eggs. They contain no meat, fish or dairy foods.

Lacto-ovo vegetarian indicates the recipes are suitable for vegetarians who are happy to eat eggs and dairy foods. They contain no meat or seafood.

Nut-free these recipes do not contain any tree nuts or peanuts.

Egg-free indicates that the recipes do not contain eggs in any form.

Gluten-free these recipes are gluten-free and are therefore suitable for coeliacs and those following a low gluten, or gluten-free diet. These recipes do not contain wheat, barley, rye or oats*.

*Oats do not contain gluten but a related protein (avenins). Most coeliac sufferers can eat oats, but a small number may also react to avenins. For this reason and because oat crops are often contaminated with wheat or other grains, the Australian Coeliac Society recommends avoiding oats to be safe. However if you are not coeliac, but are following a low gluten or gluten-free diet, you may like to include oats for their many health benefits.

Dairy-free indicates the recipes are free from dairy foods including milk, yoghurt, cream, butter and cheese.

Paleo these recipes do not contain any grains, dairy foods, seed oils, legumes (lentils, chickpeas or beans), or added refined sugars.

Sugar-free indicates the recipes do not have any added refined sugars. They may include foods that naturally contain sugars such as fruit, but no additional sugar is added in any form.

Dr Joanna McMillan
Accredited Practising Dietitian
& Nutritionist
www.drjoanna.com.au
www.getlean.com.au

KICK START
THE DAY

WHAT'S THE DIFFERENCE BETWEEN A FOOD ALLERGY AND A FOOD INTOLERANCE? AN ALLERGY IS WHERE THE BODY'S IMMUNE SYSTEM REACTS TO ALLERGENS (A SUBSTANCE THAT CAUSES AN ALLERGIC REACTION) IN THE FOOD, WHEREAS A FOOD INTOLERANCE DOES NOT INVOLVE THE IMMUNE SYSTEM.

It's crucial for anyone who has an extreme allergy to have an anaphylaxis management plan from their doctor, and to completely avoid the offending food.

Fortunately the majority of allergies to food won't trigger life-threatening reactions. Most food allergies cause reactions within the gut, or once absorbed can affect the skin, causing hives (urticaria) or eczema, and less commonly the respiratory system and sinuses.

Research is now looking at the possibility of some people having a gluten sensitivity in the absence of coeliac disease. In this case, strict avoidance of gluten is not required, and the diet is therefore less restrictive.

Coeliac disease is a severe intolerance to gluten (a protein), where even small amounts can seriously damage the wall of the intestine. There is strong genetic evidence, and gene tests are available to assess any risk. However, a definitive diagnosis, consisting of a blood test and a biopsy (where a small piece of tissue is taken from the small bowel for examination by a pathologist), is essential to know whether you must be strictly gluten free for life. Don't cut out gluten before this test, otherwise any damage to the small bowel will not be able to be seen and identified.

SELF-DIAGNOSED ALLERGIES AND INTOLERANCES ARE OFTEN INCORRECT AND YOU MAY CONTINUE TO HAVE PROBLEMS. IT'S IMPORTANT YOU ARE PROPERLY TESTED FOR BOTH FOOD ALLERGIES AND INTOLERANCES TO ENSURE YOU ARE ELIMINATING THE CORRECT FOOD. SEE A DOCTOR AND/OR DIETITIAN TO ENSURE YOU HAVE THE CORRECT DIAGNOSIS AND THE CORRECT DIET.

Many symptoms of food allergies and intolerances are similar, but only an allergy can result in a potentially life-threatening anaphylaxis. Peanuts and shellfish are amongst the most common foods to trigger severe allergic reactions.

ALLERGY FREE

WHEAT IS ALSO A CAUSE OF ALLERGIES AND INTOLERANCES. HOWEVER, IF YOU HAVE A WHEAT INTOLERANCE, YOU MAY FIND YOU ARE FINE WITH OTHER CEREALS CONTAINING GLUTEN, SUCH AS BARLEY, RYE AND OATS, AND THE SO-CALLED ANCIENT GRAINS, SPELT AND KAMUT.

If you have a number of food allergies or intolerances, make sure you don't restrict your nutrient intake along with the offending foods. Replace highly nutritious foods with others that also provide key nutrients - a dietitian can help with this. A gluten-free diet is not necessarily healthy. Many gluten-free packaged foods are heavily processed and are high in both refined starch and sugar, with a correspondingly high Glycaemic Index (GI).

Beware of food allergens hidden in mass-produced processed foods. Deciphering food labels can be tricky, but knowing what the labels mean is key to avoiding life-threating situations. Egg products may appear as albumin; dairy as lactalbumin or casein; soy as tempeh or TVP (textured vegetable protein); gluten can be found as food starches or malt; and peanuts are often used as thickeners in many sauces.

Be wary of dubious food intolerance tests. There are many available that can cost a lot of money but lack scientific evidence for their use. Seek help from reputable health professionals with experience in the area.

huevos rancheros

1 tablespoon extra virgin olive oil

1 medium brown onion (150g), chopped coarsely

250g (8 ounces) mini red capsicums (bell peppers), quartered

2 cloves garlic, crushed

2 teaspoons ground cumin

1kg (2 pounds) vine-ripened tomatoes, chopped coarsely

400g (12½ ounces) canned red kidney beans, rinsed, drained

2 tablespoons coarsely chopped fresh coriander leaves (cilantro)

100g (3 ounces) drained persian fetta, crumbled

4 free-range eggs

1 fresh green jalapeño chilli, sliced thinly

⅓ cup loosely packed fresh coriander sprigs (cilantro), extra

1 Heat oil in a large frying pan over medium heat; cook onion and capsicum, stirring, for 5 minutes or until soft. Add garlic and cumin; cook, stirring, until fragrant. Stir in tomatoes and beans; simmer, uncovered, for 20 minutes or until sauce thickens. Season to taste. Stir in coriander.

2 Meanwhile, preheat oven to 180°C/350°F; place a 1 litre (4-cup) ovenproof dish in the oven while preheating.

3 Pour hot tomato mixture into hot dish, top with fetta; make four indents in the mixture. Break eggs, one at a time, into a cup, sliding each into an indent. Sprinkle with chilli.

4 Bake for 8 minutes or until egg whites are set and the egg yolks are just beginning to set. (The cooking time will vary depending on what your ovenproof dish is made from, and may take up to 15 minutes to cook.)

5 Serve huevos rancheros topped with extra coriander.

prep + cook time 45 minutes **serves** 4
nutritional count per serving 16.7g total fat (6.2g saturated fat); 1356kJ (324 cal); 19.3g carbohydrate; 19.6g protein; 9.5g fibre

tips The tomato mixture can be made a day ahead; reheat before adding the eggs. If you can't find mini capsicums, use 1 medium-sized capsicum instead and cut into chunky pieces.
serving suggestion Serve with gluten and yeast-free flatbread.

poached eggs, mushrooms & and spinach with kumara rosti

1 medium lemon (140g)

1 fresh long red chilli, seeded, chopped finely

2 tablespoons finely chopped fresh lemon thyme

1 clove garlic, crushed

½ cup (125ml) extra virgin olive oil

4 flat mushrooms (480g), stems trimmed

2 small kumara (orange sweet potato) (600g), grated coarsely

1 tablespoon wholemeal plain (all-purpose), rice or coconut flour (see tip)

5 free-range eggs

¼ cup (60ml) olive oil

1 tablespoon white vinegar

600g (1¼ pounds) english spinach, trimmed

4 fresh thyme sprigs, extra

1 Preheat oven to 180°C/350°F.

2 Remove rind from lemon with a zester into long thin strips. Squeeze juice from lemon; you will need 2½ tablespoons juice.

3 To make lemon chilli dressing, stir rind, chilli, chopped lemon thyme, garlic and oil in a small saucepan over low heat for 5 minutes or until mixture is warm. Remove from heat; stir in juice, season to taste.

4 Place mushrooms on an oven tray. Drizzle with some of the lemon chilli dressing; season. Bake for 15 minutes or until mushrooms are tender.

5 Meanwhile, squeeze excess moisture from kumara. Combine kumara, flour and 1 egg in a medium bowl; season. Heat half the olive oil in a large frying pan over medium heat. Add a quarter of the kumara mixture, flatten with a spatula into a 13cm (5¼-inches) round; cook for 2 minutes each side or until browned and cooked through. Transfer rösti to a tray; cover with foil to keep warm. Repeat with remaining mixture to make four rösti in total, adding more oil to pan when necessary.

6 To poach eggs, half-fill a large, deep frying pan with water, add vinegar; bring to a gentle simmer. Break 1 egg into a cup. Using a wooden spoon, make a whirlpool in the water; slide egg into whirlpool. Repeat with a second egg. Cook eggs for 3 minutes or until whites are set and the yolks remain runny. Remove eggs with a slotted spoon; drain on a paper-towel-lined plate. Keep warm. Repeat poaching with remaining eggs.

7 Heat remaining olive oil in a large saucepan over medium-high heat, add spinach; cook, covered, stirring occasionally, for 2 minutes or until just wilted. Season.

8 Divide rösti among plates; top with spinach, mushrooms and eggs. Drizzle eggs with remaining lemon chilli dressing. Serve sprinkled with extra thyme sprigs and with lemon cheeks, if you like.

prep + cook time 40 minutes **serves** 4

nutritional count per serving 49.5g total fat (8.7g saturated fat); 2757kJ (615 cal); 23g carbohydrate; 7g protein; 7g fibre

tips For a paleo diet use coconut flour and for a gluten-free diet use rice flour. If you don't have a zester, you can finely grate the lemon rind instead. The secret to successful poached eggs is to use fresh eggs. As an egg ages, the white breaks down, becoming runny, and it doesn't cling to the yolk very well. Check the cartons when you buy eggs and select one with the longest use-by-date.

grilled eggs with spiced fennel and spinach

2 teaspoons olive oil

1 clove garlic, crushed

1 fresh small red thai (serrano) chilli, sliced finely

½ small fennel bulb (100g), trimmed, sliced finely (reserve fennel fronds)

100g (3 ounces) baby corn, halved

50g (1½ ounces) baby spinach leaves

2 free-range eggs

1 tablespoon finely grated parmesan

2 slices rye sourdough bread (90g), toasted

1 Preheat grill (broiler) to high.

2 Heat oil in a large ovenproof frying pan over medium heat; cook garlic, chilli, fennel and corn, stirring occasionally, for 5 minutes or until fennel is soft. Add spinach; cook, stirring, for 1 minute or until spinach has wilted.

3 Make two holes in the spinach mixture; break one egg into each hole, sprinkle with parmesan. Place under grill for 2 minutes or until eggs are cooked as desired.

4 Serve eggs and spinach mixture sprinkled with fennel fronds; accompany with toast.

prep + cook time 20 minutes **serves** 2
nutritional count per serving 18.3g total fat (4.9g saturated fat); 581kJ (378 cal); 28g carbohydrate; 21.6g protein; 7.2g fibre; 404mg sodium; low GI

tip You need an ovenproof frying pan as it goes under the grill or, cover the pan handle with a few layers of foil to protect it from the heat.

mixed mushrooms with smoked salmon, egg and seed topping

20g (¾ ounce) sunflower seeds, chopped coarsely

20g (¾ ounce) pepitas (pumpkin seeds) chopped coarsely

2½ tablespoons olive oil

600g (1¼ pounds) swiss brown mushrooms, sliced thickly

600g (1¼ pounds) oyster mushrooms

1 large clove garlic, crushed

1 fresh long red chilli, seeded, chopped finely

1 tablespoon water

2 teaspoons lemon juice

4 free-range eggs

1 tablespoon vinegar

200g (6½ ounces) smoked salmon

2 tablespoons fresh chervil leaves

1 Heat a large frying pan over medium heat. Add sunflower seeds and pepitas; cook, stirring, for 2 minutes or until seeds are toasted. Remove from pan.

2 Heat 1 tablespoon of the oil in same pan over high heat, add half the mushrooms; cook, stirring occasionally, for 4 minutes or until browned lightly. Transfer to a large bowl; cover with foil to keep warm. Repeat with another tablespoon of the oil and the remaining mushrooms.

3 Return all mushrooms to pan, stir in garlic, chilli and water; cook for 1 minute or until fragrant. Remove from heat; stir in lemon juice; season to taste. Transfer to bowl; cover with foil to keep warm.

4 Meanwhile, to poach eggs, half-fill a large, deep frying pan with water, add vinegar; bring to a gentle simmer. Break 1 egg into a cup. Using a wooden spoon, make a whirlpool in the water; slide egg into whirlpool. Repeat with a second egg. Cook eggs for 3 minutes or until whites are set and the yolks remain runny. Remove eggs with a slotted spoon; drain on a paper-towel-lined plate. Keep warm. Repeat poaching with remaining eggs.

5 Divide mushroom mixture among plates, top with eggs, smoked salmon, seed mixture and chervil; season.

prep + cook time 20 minutes **serves** 4
nutritional count per serving 24.3g total fat (4.4g saturated fat); 1596kJ (381 cal); 4.7g carbohydrate; 30.7g protein; 11.6g fibre

tip You can also scatter the eggs with sprouts, see glossary entry '*germinating sprouts*' page 235, on how to grow your own.

Sunflower seeds are packed with nutrients and are a greatsource of the antioxidantvitamin E, which plays a rolein heart health, as well asprotecting the skin from sundamage and aging. They can beeaten raw or lightly toasted, aswell as sprinkled into salads,stir-fries or on top of baked goods, such as muffins.

Quinoa, black (top) white (left) and red (see below), is cooked and eaten as a grain, but is, in fact, a seed. It's a good source of protein, contains all the essential amino acids and is high in fibre.

Red quinoa is nutritionally equal to black and white quinoa, however, it has a slightly more fibrous texture, so holds its shape better after cooking than white quinoa. It is also a little crunchier once cooked.

Pepitas, or pumpkin seeds, are rich in healthy unsaturated fats, and are packed with fibre. They are an especially good source of iron, making them a valuable addition to vegetarian and vegan diets.

Flaxseeds, also known as linseeds, are especially rich in fibre; adding just 1 tablespoon to your breakfast cereal delivers 3g fibre.

White chia seeds are nutritionally equal to black chia seeds (see below); both are fibre-rich and provide a wealth of vitamins, minerals and antioxidants.

SEEDS

The abundance of seeds and grains on offer at health-food stores and supermarkets these days is truly eye-opening. Many are gluten-free, full of protein and contain all the essential amino acids, making them a perfect food for the ever-growing population of vegetarian and vegan dieters.

Activated bukinis, or buckwheat groats, is made with buckwheat. It is gluten-free and has excellent levels of magnesium, B-group vitamins, phosphorus and zinc. It's terrific for vegetarian and vegan diets, as it is relatively rich in protein and contains all the essential amino acids.

Black chia seeds contain protein and all the essential amino acids, making them a great addition to vegetarian and vegan diets.

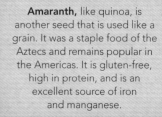

Amaranth, like quinoa, is another seed that is used like a grain. It was a staple food of the Aztecs and remains popular in the Americas. It is gluten-free, high in protein, and is an excellent source of iron and manganese.

fatteh

This recipe, which is a typical Lebanese breakfast dish, serves just two, however, it is usually served on a big plate so friends, family, and even the neighbours, can share. Double or triple the recipe to serve more.

420g (12½ ounces) canned no-added-salt chickpeas (garbanzo beans), rinsed, drained

⅓ cup (80ml) water

1 wholemeal lebanese bread (80g)

3 teaspoons olive oil

1½ cups (420g) low-fat plain yoghurt

1 clove garlic, crushed

¼ cup (40g) pine nuts, toasted

¼ teaspoon sumac

1 Combine chickpeas and the water in a small saucepan over medium heat. Bring to the boil, reduce heat to low; simmer, covered, for 5 minutes. Using a potato masher, roughly mash chickpeas; cover to keep warm.

2 Preheat grill (broiler) to medium. Brush bread with oil; place on an oven tray. Grill both sides until bread is dry and crisp (be careful not to burn the bread). Break bread into pieces.

3 Combine yoghurt and garlic in a small bowl.

4 To serve, divide bread pieces between two plates; spoon over warm chickpea mash. Top with yoghurt mixture; sprinkle with pine nuts and with sumac. Serve immediately.

prep + cook time 15 minutes **serves** 2

nutritional count per serving 25g total fat (2.8g saturated fat); 2350kJ (561 cal); 50.9g carbohydrate; 27.1g protein; 10.2g fibre; 347mg sodium; low GI

tips If you find the chickpea mixture too thick, add an extra teaspoon or two of hot water. If you prefer, crisp the bread in a 200°C/400°F oven for about 5 minutes.

toast with avocado, tahini and sumac tomatoes

3 medium roma (egg) tomatoes (225g), halved lengthways

½ teaspoon sumac

cooking-oil spray

½ clove garlic, crushed

¼ cup (70g) low-fat plain yoghurt

1 tablespoon unhulled tahini (sesame seed paste)

1 teaspoon lemon juice

½ small avocado (100g)

2 slices wholegrain sourdough bread (120g), toasted

1 Preheat oven to 180°C/350°F. Grease and line a small oven tray with baking paper.

2 Place tomato on tray, cut-side up; sprinkle with sumac, spray lightly with oil. Roast for 30 minutes or until tomato is softened.

3 Place garlic, yoghurt, tahini and juice in a small bowl; whisk to combine.

4 Spread half the avocado thickly over each toast slice. Spoon tahini mixture over avocado and top with tomatoes.

prep + cook time 40 minutes **serves** 2

nutritional count per serving 17.4g total fat (3g saturated fat); 1490kJ (356 cal); 33.5g carbohydrate; 12.2g protein; 7.2g fibre; 371mg sodium; low GI

tips We cut the sourdough into 1.5cm (¾-inch) slices. Cook extra sumac tomatoes and keep them in the fridge and use as a delicious addition in pasta, salads and sandwiches. Store them in an airtight container for up to a week.

strawberry and ricotta pancakes with honey

⅓ cup (80g) low-fat ricotta

2 free-range eggs, separated

2 tablespoons caster (superfine) sugar

1 teaspoon vanilla extract

¼ cup (35g) buckwheat flour

⅓ cup (50g) wholemeal self-raising flour

¼ cup (45g) finely chopped strawberries

cooking-oil spray

150g (4½ ounces) strawberries, extra, quartered

1 tablespoon coarsely chopped almonds

2 teaspoons honey

1 Whisk ricotta, egg yolks, sugar and extract in a small bowl. Stir in sifted flours and finely chopped strawberries.

2 Beat egg whites in a small bowl with an electric mixer until soft peaks form. Fold through ricotta mixture in two batches.

3 Spray a medium frying pan with oil; heat over medium heat. Spoon ¼ cup of batter into pan; cook pancake for 3 minutes each side or until golden. Repeat with remaining mixture.

4 Serve pancakes with extra strawberries and nuts; drizzle with honey.

prep + cook time 20 minutes **serves** 2

nutritional count per serving 14.5g total fat (4.2g saturated fat); 1812kJ (433 cal); 57.5g carbohydrate; 16.2g protein; 5.7g fibre; 291mg sodium; low GI

tips You may need to slightly spread the pancake batter with the back of a spoon if it doesn't spread when you add it to the frying pan. These pancakes are also great for dessert. You can make little pancakes, if you prefer, using just 1 tablespoon of mixture. Swap the strawberries for bananas, if you like.

serving suggestion Dust each serve with ¼ teaspoon icing (confectioners') sugar.

ricotta and basil pancakes with tomato and rocket salad

300g (9½ ounces) baby truss roma (egg) tomatoes

2 tablespoons extra virgin olive oil

1 cup (240g) ricotta

1 egg

1¼ cups (310ml) milk

1¼ cups (185g) self-raising flour

½ cup coarsely chopped fresh basil

¼ cup (20g) grated parmesan

30g (1 ounce) butter

1 tablespoon white balsamic vinegar

250g (8 ounces) rocket (arugula)

½ small red onion (50g), sliced thinly

1 Preheat oven to 220°C/425°F. Place tomatoes in a small baking dish; drizzle with half the oil, season. Roast for 10 minutes or until skins just split.

2 Whisk ricotta and egg in a medium bowl until combined. Whisk in milk, then flour. Stir in basil and parmesan; season.

3 Melt a little of the butter in a large frying pan over medium heat. Pour ¼-cups of mixture into pan, allowing room for spreading. Cook pancakes for 2 minutes each side or until golden and cooked through. Stack pancakes; cover to keep warm.

4 Wipe out pan with paper towel; repeat with remaining butter and batter to make 12 pancakes in total.

5 Drizzle remaining oil and vinegar over rocket and onion in a medium bowl, season to taste; toss gently to combine.

6 Serve warm pancakes topped with rocket mixture, tomatoes and any remaining dressing.

prep + cook time 45 minutes **serves** 4

nutritional count per serving 21.7g total fat (11g saturated fat); 1920kJ (459 cal); 44.5g carbohydrate; 19.2g protein; 4.1g fibre

tip Wipe the pan clean with paper towel between each batch of pancakes so they don't over-brown.

strawberry and passionfruit breakfast trifle

2 Weet-Bix (50g), broken into chunks

½ cup (40g) All-Bran cereal

⅓ cup (80ml) fresh passionfruit pulp

1 cup (280g) low-fat plain yoghurt or soy yoghurt (see tips)

140g (1½ ounces) strawberries, sliced thinly

1 Layer half each of the Weet-Bix and All-Bran in two 1¼-cup (310ml) serving glasses. Top with half each of the passionfruit, yoghurt and strawberries.

2 Repeat layering with remaining Weet-Bix, All-Bran and yoghurt. Top with remaining strawberries and drizzle with remaining passionfruit.

prep time 5 minutes **serves** 2

nutritional count per serving 2g total fat (0.5g saturated fat) 722kJ (172 cal); 36.1g carbohydrate;16.2g protein; 15.5g fibre; 411mg sodium; low GI

tips For vegan diets, substitute coconut milk yoghurt or soy milk yoghurt for cow's milk yoghurt. Assemble the trifle when ready to eat so the cereals keep their crunch. You will need about 4 passionfruit. You can make the trifle with any seasonal fruit combination or even with canned fruit in natural juices. Canned pears and frozen raspberries work well together.

muesli with poached pears and sheep's milk yoghurt

Eating a healthy breakfast with a good mix of slow-release carbs and protein will help to keep your blood sugar levels in check for the rest of the day. You can skip the poached pear part of this recipe if you like, and top with a mix of fresh or frozen berries instead.

⅓ cup (95g) almond butter

⅓ cup (80ml) pure maple syrup

2 cups (180g) rolled oats

1 cup (50g) flaked coconut

½ cup (80g) flaked almonds

¼ cup (50g) pepitas (pumpkin seeds)

¼ cup (35g) sunflower seeds

¼ cup (20g) quinoa flakes

¼ cup (35g) rolled amaranth or rolled rye

2 tablespoons black or white chia seeds

1 cup (160g) dried unsweetened cranberries

6 small corella pears (600g)

2 cups (500ml) apple juice

2 cups (500ml) water

1½ cups (420g) sheep's milk yoghurt

1 Preheat oven to 160°C/325°F. Line a large roasting pan with baking paper.

2 Stir almond butter and syrup in a small saucepan over low heat just until combined.

3 Combine oats, coconut, nuts, pepitas, seeds, quinoa and amaranth in a large bowl. Pour syrup mixture over dry ingredients; working quickly, stir to coat ingredients in mixture.

4 Spread muesli, in an even layer, in pan. Bake for 15 minutes. Remove from oven; stir well. Bake for a further 5 minutes or until oats are golden. Cool for 10 minutes; stir in chia seeds and cranberries.

5 Meanwhile, peel, halve and core pears, leaving stalks intact. Place pears in a medium saucepan with juice and the water; bring to the boil. Reduce heat to low; cover pears with a round of baking paper, simmer for 8 minutes or until tender.

6 Serve muesli topped with yoghurt and poached pears. If you like, drizzle with honey.

prep + cook time 45 minutes **serves** 6

nutritional count per serving 36.8g total fat (9g saturated fat); 2862kJ (684 cal); 61g carbohydrate; 19g protein; 16g fibre

tips Similarly to quinoa, amaranth is treated as a grain. You will be able to find the ingredients for this muesli either in the health food aisle at most supermarkets or health food stores. The muesli will keep in an airtight container for up to 1 month.

chia and almond toasted muesli

½ cup (45g) rolled oats

1 tablespoon chia seeds

2 tablespoons coarsely chopped almonds

¼ teaspoon mixed spice

2 teaspoons dark agave nectar

1 tablespoon sunflower seeds

1 tablespoon LSA (ground linseeds, sunflower seeds and almonds)

1 medium kiwi fruit (85g), sliced thinly

50g (1½ ounces) strawberries, sliced thinly

1 medium banana (200g), sliced thinly

⅓ cup (95g) low-fat plain yoghurt (see tips)

½ cup (125ml) skim milk (see tips)

1 Preheat oven to 200°C/400°F.

2 Grease and line an oven tray with baking paper. Combine oats, chia, nuts and spice on tray. Drizzle with nectar; toss well. Bake muesli for 10 minutes or until mixture is browned lightly. Cool on tray.

3 Transfer muesli to a medium bowl; stir through seeds and LSA.

4 Divide muesli evenly into two bowls; top with fruit and yoghurt. Serve each with ¼ cup milk.

prep + cook time 20 minutes (+ cooling) **serves** 2 (makes 1 cup)
nutritional count per serving 16g total fat (1.5g saturated fat); 1621kJ (387 cal); 40.5g carbohydrate; 15.2g protein; 9.6g fibre; 78mg sodium; low GI

tips Make double or triple the muesli recipe and store it in an airtight container in the fridge for up to 3 months. While the muesli is suitable for vegans you will need to serve it with non-diary alternatives to milk and yoghurt. You can try rice or almond milk and either coconut milk or soy yoghurt instead.

Coconut flour is a low carbohydrate, high fibre, gluten-free flour made from fresh dried coconut flesh. It has a sweetish taste and is suitable for those on a paleo diet.

Coconut flesh gives you a fibre boost, but is not as rich in vitamins and minerals as tree nuts (almond, brazil, cashew etc).

Coconut sugar is not made from coconuts, but from the sap of the blossoms of the coconut palm tree. The refined sap looks a little like raw or light brown sugar, and has a similar caramel flavour. It also has the same amount of kilojoules as regular table (white) sugar.

Coconut cream comes from the first pressing of the coconut flesh, without the addition of water; the second pressing (less rich) is sold as coconut milk. Look for coconut cream labelled as 100% coconut, without added emulsifiers.

Coconut oil is extracted from the coconut flesh so you don't get any of the fibre, protein or carbohydrates present in the whole coconut. The best quality is virgin coconut oil, which is the oil pressed from the dried coconut flesh, and doesn't include the use of solvents or other refining processes.

Coconut flakes are a good source of protein, are low in carbohydrates and high in fibre. Sprinkle over muesli, porridge or use on cakes.

Coconut water is the liquid from the centre of a young green coconut. It has fewer kilojoules than fruit juice, with no fat or protein. There are sugars present, but these are slowly absorbed giving coconut water a low GI.

COCONUT

Coconut and its natural food products are currently all the rage. Once relegated to the 'bad fat' basket, it has been found that coconut contains 'medium chain saturated fats': these are burned more readily for energy than other fats, so are less likely to be stored as fat.

Shredded coconut is thin strips of dried coconut. Add it to muesli, sprinkle over porridge, or use it in cakes and slices.

Young coconuts are coconuts that are not fully mature. As a coconut ages, the amount of juice inside decreases, until it eventually disappears and is replaced by air.

quinoa porridge

½ cup (100g) white quinoa, rinsed, drained

1½ cups (375ml) water

½ cup (125ml) skim milk or almond milk

1 medium apple (150g), grated coarsely

100g (3 ounces) red seedless grapes, halved

2 tablespoons pistachios, toasted, chopped coarsely

1 tablespoon honey or pure maple syrup

1 Combine quinoa and the water in a small saucepan; bring to the boil. Reduce heat; simmer, covered, for 10 minutes. Add milk; cook, covered, for a further 5 minutes or until quinoa is tender.

2 Stir in apple and half the grapes.

3 Serve porridge topped with nuts and remaining grapes; drizzle with honey.

prep + cook time 20 minutes serves 2

nutritional count per serving 8.9g total fat (1g saturated fat); 642kJ (392 cal); 63g carbohydrate; 12.2g protein; 5.6g fibre; 53mg sodium; low GI.

tips We used a pink lady apple in this recipe. Most quinoa comes rinsed, but it's a good habit to rinse it yourself under cold water until the water runs clear, then drain it. This removes any remaining outer coating, which has a bitter taste. Quinoa absorbs a lot of liquid. Depending how you like your porridge, add a little boiling water at the end of step 1 to thin it out.

bircher muesli

2 cups (180g) gluten-free quick oats

1 large green apple (200g), grated coarsely

½ cup (125ml) apple juice

⅓ cup (80ml) orange juice

½ cup (140g) vanilla soy yoghurt

1 tablespoon caster (superfine) sugar

1 tablespoon finely grated orange rind

½ teaspoon ground cinnamon

¼ teaspoon ground cardamom

125g (4 ounces) blueberries

1 Combine oats, apple, juices, yoghurt, sugar, rind, cinnamon and cardamom in a large bowl. Cover; refrigerate for 1 hour or overnight.

2 Add blueberries; stir to combine. Top with extra rind to serve, if you like.

prep time 15 minutes (+ refrigeration) **serves** 4
nutritional count per serving 2.1g total fat (0.3g saturated fat); 747kJ (178 cal); 34.3g carbohydrate; 3.9g protein; 3.9g fibre

tip Use greek-style yoghurt if you don't have a dairy allergy.

omelette with asparagus and mint

1 baby new potato (40g), cut into 5mm (¼-inch) cubes

170g (5½ ounces) asparagus, trimmed

1 cup (120g) frozen peas

2 free-range eggs

¹/₃ cup coarsely chopped fresh mint leaves

1 tablespoon olive oil

2 slices rye sourdough bread (90g), toasted

1 Cook potato in a small saucepan of boiling water for 3 minutes; add asparagus and peas, cook for a further minute or until asparagus is bright green and potato is tender; drain. When cool enough to handle, cut the asparagus in half crossways; finely slice the stem ends crossways.

2 Lightly whisk eggs in a medium bowl; stir in potato, peas, mint and chopped asparagus ends.

3 Heat half the oil in a small non-stick frying pan on high; cook half the egg mixture for about 2 minutes, pulling in the egg with a spatula to help it cook quickly. Fold over; slide onto a warm serving plate. Repeat with remaining oil and egg mixture to make a second omelette.

4 Top omelettes with remaining asparagus; serve with toast.

prep + cook time 20 minutes **makes** 2
nutritional count per serving 15.8g total fat (3.4g saturated fat); 1400kJ (335 cal); 27.7g carbohydrate; 16.3g protein; 8.8g fibre; 275mg sodium; low GI

tips If you are pressed for time, make one big omelette in a medium frying pan. You can change the filling depending on the seasonal vegetables available - try adding pumpkin or broccolini.

LUNCH
ON
THE GO

Vegan diets contain no animal foods of any kind. That means no meat, no fish, no seafood, no eggs and no dairy foods. The diet is entirely made up of plant foods. The decision to follow a vegan diet is almost always an ethical one, although some religions and other spiritual teachings may promote a vegan diet.

PLANT-BASED DIETS ARE GAINING MORE AND MORE SUPPORT WITH NUTRITIONAL RESEARCH SHOWING STRONG EVIDENCE THAT THESE TYPES OF DIETS CAN REDUCE THE RISK OF HEART DISEASE AND TYPE 2 DIABETES AS WELL AS MANY TYPES OF CANCER. HOWEVER, THIS IS MOST LIKELY TO BE DUE TO THE HIGH INTAKE OF PLANT FOODS RATHER THAN THE EXCLUSION OF ANIMAL FOODS.

Consuming more raw foods is a great way to boost gut health, especially colon health. The body has to work hard to break down the plant cell walls, meaning more raw foods reach the colon intact. The resident bacteria break them down instead; this results in antioxidants being released, which helps to protect the cells of the colon.

Amino acids are the building blocks of protein; they are vital to life and have an influence on every function in the body. Animal foods contain all eight essential amino acids that we need, however, plant foods are usually low in or lacking at least one. So, if you're on a vegetarian diet, eat complementary plant foods: think of including foods from the following groups each day – legumes (lentils, beans and chickpeas), nuts and seeds, wholegrains and vegies.

IF YOU ARE FOLLOWING, OR WANT TO FOLLOW, A VEGAN DIET, PLANT FOODS CAN PROVIDE ALL OF THE PROTEIN YOU NEED, HOWEVER, FOR THIS TO OCCUR YOU MUST COMBINE DIFFERENT FOODS TOGETHER.

Consuming a food rich in vitamin C boosts your absorption of the iron present in plant foods. Try pairing a raw salad made with leafy greens and capsicum, with a bean casserole, or have a fresh fruit salad for dessert after a tofu stir-fry.

VITAMIN B12 IS ONLY FOUND IN ANIMAL FOODS, SO IF YOU ARE FOLLOWING A VEGAN DIET YOU MUST TAKE A SUPPLEMENT OR ENSURE YOU CONSUME FOODS FORTIFIED WITH THIS VITAMIN.

While eating some food raw is beneficial, be wary of following a completely raw diet. Cooking may result in the loss of some nutrients, but it makes others more available and is necessary for most grains and legumes. The best approach is to combine raw and cooked food to gain all the benefits.

RAW FOOD

Soy is a particularly useful food as it provides all of the essential amino acids. Rather than relying on processed soy – used in commercially produced high-protein bars, shakes and packaged vegetarian foods – choose traditional soy foods such as tofu, tempeh, edamame and whole soy milk.

Iron, zinc and calcium are present in many plant foods, but they are much harder to absorb from these sources compared to animal foods. Ensure you consume a wide variety of plant foods including leafy greens, legumes, nuts, seeds and wholegrains over refined grains.

MANY TRADITIONAL FOOD COMBINATIONS AROUND THE WORLD MARRY COMPLEMENTARY PLANT PROTEINS, AND HAVE DONE SO FOR THOUSANDS OF YEARS. IN INDIA DHAL IS CONSUMED WITH RICE, IN MEXICO BEANS ARE COMBINED WITH CORN TORTILLAS, IN AFRICA CASSAVA IS COMBINED WITH BEANS, AND SO ON.

romesco sauce with eggplant and zucchini

olive-oil spray

2 medium eggplant (900g), sliced on the diagonal

4 zucchini (480g), sliced thinly lengthways

⅓ cup (55g) blanched almonds, roasted, chopped coarsely

⅓ cup (45g) skinless roasted hazelnuts, chopped coarsely

¼ cup fresh flat-leaf parsley leaves, torn

romesco sauce

2 medium red capsicum (bell peppers) (400g)

1 medium tomato (150g)

2 tablespoons extra virgin olive oil

2 cloves garlic

2 teaspoons sweet paprika

½ cup (80g) blanched almonds, roasted

½ cup (70g) skinless roasted hazelnuts

2 tablespoons sherry or red wine vinegar

¼ cup (60ml) water

1 Make romesco sauce.

2 Preheat a grill pan to high. Spray vegetables with olive oil; season with salt. Cook vegetables, in batches, for 4 minutes each side until tender and lightly charred.

3 Layer vegetables on a platter; top with nuts and parsley. Serve with romesco sauce.

romesco sauce Roast capsicums and tomato directly over a gas flame on stove-top, turning until charred (or roast under a hot grill (broiler) or in a grill pan, turning until charred). Wrap individually in foil. Peel away skins. Chop capsicum and tomato; keep separated. Heat half the oil in a medium frying pan over medium heat; cook capsicum and garlic, stirring occasionally, for 3 minutes or until capsicum is soft. Add tomato and paprika; cook for 3 minutes or until tomato softens. Process nuts until chopped finely; add capsicum mixture, sherry and the water, process until smooth. Season to taste.

prep + cook time 35 minutes (+ cooling) **serves** 4
nutritional count per serving 19.4g total fat (0.9g saturated fat); 1135kJ (271 cal); 8.9g carbohydrate; 8.4g protein; 10g fibre

tips Romesco is a traditional northern Spanish sauce, much like pesto in texture, made from a mixture of nuts and fire-roasted capsicum that often accompanies seafood or a local roasted Catalonian spring onion. It is also delicious with grilled meats. The sauce can be stored in an airtight container in the fridge for up to 1 week. To take to work, layer the ingredients in a takeaway container; keep refrigerated.

Lemon thyme has a lemony scent due to the high level of citral, which is an oil also found in lemon, orange, verbena and lemon grass. Crush the leaves before using.

Rosemary is a rich source of antioxidants, and has beneficial effects on brain and eye health.

Flat-leaf parsley is packed with nutrients including carotenoids, which reduce the risk of macular degeneration of the eye, a common cause of blindness.

Berries and cream mint is so-named because its leaves have a sweet berry and mint flavour.

Mint has strong antioxidant properties, and has been studied for its positive effects on the gut. It's also a well-known breath freshener.

Sage has been shown to help reduce the loss of minerals from bone and to help boost long-term memory retention.

Bay Leaf has been used for its antioxidant, anti-bacterial, anti-inflammatory and anti-fungal properties.

Oregano is packed full of antioxidants.

Coriander's fresh leaves have good antioxidant properties and are a rich source of vitamin K.

HERBS

Using herbs brings a wealth of benefits; they give an added depth of flavour to food, boost your intake of beneficial plant compounds, including antioxidants, and many have particular medicinal effects.

Basil has anti-inflammatory effects, as well as containing vitamin A, folate, vitamin C and several minerals. Thai basil, with its aniseed flavour, is found in Asian dishes.

Thyme is another herb with good antioxidant properties. It also has shown to be beneficial in maintaining strong bones.

yellow dhal with spinach

60g (2 ounces) ghee or olive oil

1 teaspoon cumin seeds

1 teaspoon ground turmeric

¾ teaspoon ground chilli

2 shallots (50g), sliced thinly

2 cloves garlic, crushed

1 teaspoon finely grated fresh ginger

2 long fresh green chillies, sliced thinly

200g (6½ ounces) yellow lentils (channa dhal)

1.25 litres (5 cups) water

60g (2 ounces) baby spinach leaves

1 Heat ghee in a large saucepan over medium heat; cook spices, stirring, for 1 minute or until fragrant.

2 Add shallots, garlic, ginger and half the chilli; cook, stirring, for 3 minutes or until softened.

3 Meanwhile, wash lentils under running water until water runs clear; drain well. Add lentils to pan; stir until combined. Add the water; cover, bring to the boil. Reduce heat to medium-low; simmer, covered, for 30 minutes or until lentils are soft and have broken down, stirring occasionally.

4 Add spinach; stir until wilted. Season to taste. Serve dhal topped with remaining chilli.

prep + cook time 40 minutes **serves** 4

nutritional count per serving 16.5g total fat (10g saturated fat); 1237kJ (296 cal); 20.9g carbohydrate; 13.3g protein; 8.5g fibre

tips Add more water if the dhal is too thick. You could replace 3 cups of the water with vegetable stock, if you like. To take dhal to work, transport in an airtight, microwavable container; keep refrigerated. Microwave to reheat.

serving suggestion Serve with roti or gluten-free flat bread.

vegetable larb

2 tablespoons fish sauce or gluten-free tamari

2 tablespoons lime juice

½ teaspoon dried chilli flakes

1 medium beetroot (beet) (160g), peeled, cut into 5mm (¼-inch) pieces

1 large carrot (180g), unpeeled, cut into 5mm (¼-inch) pieces

160g (5 ounces) snake beans, cut into 5mm (¼-inch) pieces

1 lebanese cucumber (130g), halved lengthways

¼ cup (50g) jasmine rice (see tips)

200g (6½ ounces) small cherry tomatoes, halved

3 green onions (scallions), sliced thinly

½ cup finely chopped fresh mint

2 tablespoons finely chopped fresh thai basil or coriander (cilantro)

⅓ cup (45g) roasted unsalted peanuts, chopped finely (see tips)

1 medium butter (boston) lettuce, leaves separated

1 Preheat oven to 180°C/350°F.

2 Combine fish sauce, juice and chilli flakes in a large bowl.

3 Combine beetroot and 1 tablespoon of the dressing in a small bowl. Combine carrot, snake beans and 2 tablespoons of the dressing in a medium bowl. Remove seeds from cucumber; cut into 5mm (¼-inch) pieces. Add cucumber to remaining dressing in large bowl. Cover each bowl with plastic wrap; stand vegetables for 15 minutes.

4 Meanwhile, place rice on an oven tray; roast for 12 minutes or until golden. Process rice in a small food processor (or crush with a mortar and pestle) until very finely crushed.

5 Add tomatoes to cucumber mixture with onion, herbs, ground rice, carrot mixture and half the nuts. Strain beetroot mixture through a sieve, add to larb; toss gently to combine.

6 Serve larb with lettuce leaves, sprinkled with remaining nuts.

prep + cook time 30 minutes (+ standing)
serves 4 as a side dish
nutritional count per serving 5.8g total fat (0.8g saturated fat); 781kJ (187 cal); 21.2g carbohydrate; 7.8g protein; 8.1g fibre

tips You will need about half a bunch of snake beans for this recipe. For paleo, substitute sesame seeds for rice; roast for 5 minutes or until golden, and substitute roasted almonds for peanuts. To take the salad to work, transport in an airtight container; keep refrigerated.

Farro is the Italian name for 'emmer', an ancient wheat variety and one of the first grains ever to be cultivated. It's available in wholegrain form, retaining the majority of nutrients and fibre.

Hulled millet is a small gluten-free grain with a hard hull that is removed before using. It has a slightly nutty, corn-like flavour. It is a popular cereal in Africa and India where it is often used to make flatbread.

Spelt is another ancient grain making a comeback. It is high in fibre, protein, vitamins and minerals, and has a mild nutty flavour.

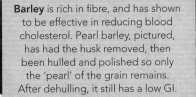

Barley is rich in fibre, and has shown to be effective in reducing blood cholesterol. Pearl barley, pictured, has had the husk removed, then been hulled and polished so only the 'pearl' of the grain remains. After dehulling, it still has a low GI.

ANCIENT GRAINS

Grown for centuries by people around the world, many ancient grains fell by the wayside as ease of harvesting, uniform growth and a grain that resulted in the right kind of flour to make bread, pasta or other baked goods grew more popular. Now, however, they're making a comeback.

Freekeh is an ancient grain made from roasted young green wheat. Nutritionally it has a low GI, four times the fibre of brown rice, and is higher in protein than regular wheat.

Teff (teff flour, pictured) is a tiny grain high in resistant starch, which promotes the growth of beneficial bacteria in the gut. It is gluten-free, and is especially high in calcium, which is terrific for those on dairy-free diets.

mediterranean grain salad with honey cumin labne

¾ cup (150g) brown rice

½ cup (100g) french-style green lentils

½ cup (100g) red or white quinoa, rinsed, drained

1 cup (250ml) water

1 small red onion (100g), chopped finely

2 tablespoons pepitas (pumpkin seeds), toasted

2 tablespoons sunflower seeds, toasted

2 tablespoons pine nuts, toasted

2 tablespoons salted baby capers, rinsed, drained

½ cup (80g) dried currants

1 cup firmly packed fresh flat-leaf parsley leaves

1 cup firmly packed fresh coriander (cilantro) leaves

¼ cup (60ml) lemon juice

⅓ cup (80ml) olive oil

1 teaspoon cumin seeds, toasted

1 cup (280g) labne

1½ tablespoons honey

½ cup (40g) flaked almonds, roasted

1 Cook rice and lentils, separately, in large saucepans of boiling water for 25 minutes or until tender; drain, rinse well.

2 Place quinoa in a small saucepan with the water; bring to the boil. Reduce heat to low; simmer, covered, for 10 minutes or until tender. Drain.

3 Combine rice, lentils and quinoa in a large bowl. Add onion, seeds, pine nuts, capers, currants, herbs, juice and oil; stir until well combined.

4 Stir cumin seeds into labne in a small bowl.

5 Serve salad on plates or a large platter; top with spoonfuls of labne, drizzle with honey and sprinkle with almonds.

prep + cook time 1 hour **serves** 6
nutritional count per serving 28.7g total fat (4.2g saturated fat); 2325kJ (555 cal); 56g carbohydrate; 15.5g protein; 8.2g fibre

tips Roast all nuts and seeds together on an oven tray (place the cumin seeds on a small piece of foil to keep them separate), in a 180°C/350°F oven for 8 minutes, stirring halfway through cooking time.

Labne is yoghurt that has been drained of whey. You can buy it from supermarkets or, to make your own labne: stir 1 teaspoon sea salt flakes into 500g (1 pound) greek-style yoghurt in a small bowl. Line a sieve with two layers of muslin or a clean chux cloth; place sieve over a deep bowl or jug. Spoon yoghurt mixture into sieve, gather cloth and tie into a ball with kitchen string. Place in the fridge for 24 hours or until thick, gently squeezing occasionally to encourage the liquid to drain. Discard liquid. Roll or shape tablespoons of labne into balls.

To take salad to work, transport in an airtight container; keep refrigerated.

spiced carrot soup with smoked almonds

1 tablespoon extra virgin olive oil

2 medium brown onions (300g), chopped coarsely

1 teaspoon finely grated fresh ginger

2 teaspoons ground cumin

1 teaspoon ground coriander

½ cinnamon stick

1kg (2 pounds) carrots, chopped coarsely

2 cups (500ml) vegetable stock

3 cups (750ml) water

¾ cup (200g) greek-style yoghurt (optional)

2 cloves garlic, crushed (optional)

½ small red onion (50g), sliced thinly lengthways

¼ cup (40g) coarsely chopped smoked almonds

8 sprigs fresh coriander (cilantro)

1 Heat oil in a large saucepan over medium heat; cook brown onion, stirring, until soft.

2 Add ginger, cumin, ground coriander and cinnamon to the pan; cook, stirring, until fragrant. Add carrot, stock and the water; bring to the boil. Reduce heat to low; simmer, covered, for 20 minutes or until carrot is soft. Remove cinnamon stick. Stand soup for 10 minutes.

3 Meanwhile, combine yoghurt and garlic in a small bowl.

4 Blend soup, in batches, until smooth (or use a stick blender). Return soup to pan; stir over medium heat until hot, season.

5 Ladle soup into serving bowls; top with yoghurt mixture, red onion, nuts and fresh coriander.

prep + cook time 45 minutes **serves** 4

nutritional count per serving 14.5g total fat (3.3g saturated fat); 1190kJ (284 cal); 24g carbohydrate; 8.9g protein; 11.7g fibre

tip To take soup to work, transport in an airtight, microwavable container; keep refrigerated. Microwave to reheat.

1

NUT- AND GLUTEN-FREE

smoked trout & avocado rolls

Cut a lebanese cucumber in half crossways; cut one half into ribbons using a vegetable peeler. Coarsely grate remaining cucumber and squeeze out excess moisture; combine grated cucumber in a bowl with 2 tablespoons low-fat plain yoghurt and 1 teaspoon ground fennel. Cut 2 gluten-free bread rolls (or soy and linseed sourdough) in half; toast cut sides. Divide half a small sliced avocado, 60g (2oz) sliced smoked ocean trout and 1 teaspoon dill sprigs evenly between roll bases. Top roll tops evenly with the cucumber ribbons and cucumber yoghurt mixture. Sandwich bread rolls together to serve.

prep time 10 minutes **serves** 2
nutritional count per serving 14.5g total fat (2.7g saturated fat); 2224kJ (531 cal); 70.4g carbohydrate; 24.4g protein; 9.1g fibre
tip If ground fennel is unavailable, grind the fennel seeds in a mortar and pestle or a mini food processor.

(recipes pictured pages 64-65)

2

GLUTEN- AND DAIRY-FREE

chicken & pumpkin rolls

Preheat oven to 220°C/425°F. Line an oven tray with baking paper. Place 200g (6½oz) coarsely chopped pumpkin onto tray. Spray with cooking oil and sprinkle with 1 teaspoon dukkah. Bake for 25 minutes or until tender; mash roughly with a fork. Cut 2 gluten-free bread rolls (or wholemeal sourdough) in half; toast cut sides. Divide pumpkin and 1 tablespoon radish sprouts evenly between roll bases. Combine 1 teaspoon macadamia oil and ½ teaspoon dukkah and drizzle evenly over sprouts. Top roll tops evenly with 20g (¾oz) baby spinach leaves and 125g (4oz) sliced smoked chicken breast. Sandwich bread rolls together to serve.

prep + cook time 30 minutes **serves** 2
nutritional count per serving 11.5g total fat (2.2g saturated fat); 2052kJ (490 cal); 58g carbohydrate; 32.7g protein; 11.3g fibre

3

NUT-FREE AND
LACTO-VEGETARIAN

mushroom &
labne rolls

Roughly chop 80g (2½oz) each of swiss brown and button mushrooms. Lightly spray a large frying pan with cooking oil. Cook mushrooms, 1 crushed garlic clove and 2 teaspoons fresh thyme leaves, over medium heat, for 5 minutes or until browned. Cut 2 seeded sourdough rolls in half; toast cut sides. Divide 3 tablespoons labne and the mushroom mixture evenly between roll bases; evenly drizzle with 2 teaspoons of olive oil. Top roll tops with 2 radicchio leaves each. Sandwich bread rolls together to serve.

prep + cook time 15 minutes **serves** 2
nutritional count per serving 10.3g total fat (1.8g saturated fat); 2033kJ (486 cal); 74.7g carbohydrate; 17.4g protein; 11.4g fibre

tip Labne is a cheese made from strained yoghurt. You can find it in supermarkets, or make your own (see tips page 59).

4

LACTO-OVO VEGETARIAN

middle-eastern
egg sandwiches

Mash 2 extra large hard-boiled eggs with a fork in a medium bowl. Stir in ¼ cup reduced-fat cottage cheese and 1 tablespoon pistachio dukkah. Divide ¼ thinly sliced small red onion, egg mixture and 2 teaspoons micro cress evenly over 2 slices of toasted rye sourdough. Divide 25g (¾oz) watercress sprigs between another 2 slices toasted rye sourdough. Sandwich bread slices together to serve.

prep time 10 minutes **serves** 2
nutritional count per serving 11.9g total fat (3.1g saturated fat); 2263kJ (541 cal); 76.3g carbohydrate; 26.4g protein; 9.5g fibre

tips We've used dukkah but you could add curry powder instead for a classic egg sandwich. Pistachio dukkah is available from most major supermarkets in the spice aisle. Store remaining watercress in the fridge with its stems in water, like flowers, for 2 days.

1

SANDWICH TOGETHER

SANDWICH TOGETHER

2

SANDWICH TOGETHER

3

SANDWICH TOGETHER

4

salmon and quinoa salad

1 cup (200g) quinoa, rinsed, drained

3 cups (750ml) water

200g (6½ ounces) snow peas, trimmed, sliced thinly lengthways

1 lebanese cucumber (130g), halved lengthways, sliced thinly crossways

½ cup loosely packed small fresh mint leaves

1 tablespoon thinly sliced lemon rind (see tips)

¼ cup (60ml) lemon juice

2 tablespoons olive oil

150g (4½ ounces) hot-smoked salmon, skinned, flaked coarsely

1 Combine quinoa and the water in a large saucepan; bring to the boil. Reduce heat to low; cook, covered, for 15 minutes or until liquid is absorbed and quinoa is tender. Rinse, drain well.
2 Place snow peas in a heatproof bowl. Pour over boiling water, stand for 2 minutes; refresh under cold running water, drain well.
3 Combine quinoa, snow peas, cucumber and mint in a large bowl; toss to combine, season to taste. Add combined juice and oil; toss to coat. Serve salad topped with salmon and rind.

prep + cook time 25 minutes **serves** 4
nutritional count per serving 16.2g total fat (2.6g saturated fat); 1556kJ (372 cal); 35g carbohydrate; 19.3g protein; 5.1g fibre

tips Use a zesting tool for the lemon rind. You can use freshly cooked salmon, coarsely flaked smoked trout or smoked chicken as an alternative to the hot-smoked salmon. Add asparagus and snow pea sprouts for extra crunch. To take salad to work, transport in an airtight container; keep refrigerated.

Mussels have more iron than red meat! Shellfish is one of the best dietary sources of iodine, essential for brain development in children.

Whiting have a delicate, sweet flavour and medium-textured, flaky flesh. King George whiting (left) have dark spots on its side. School whiting (right) have a distinct silvery stripe running down the middle of their body.

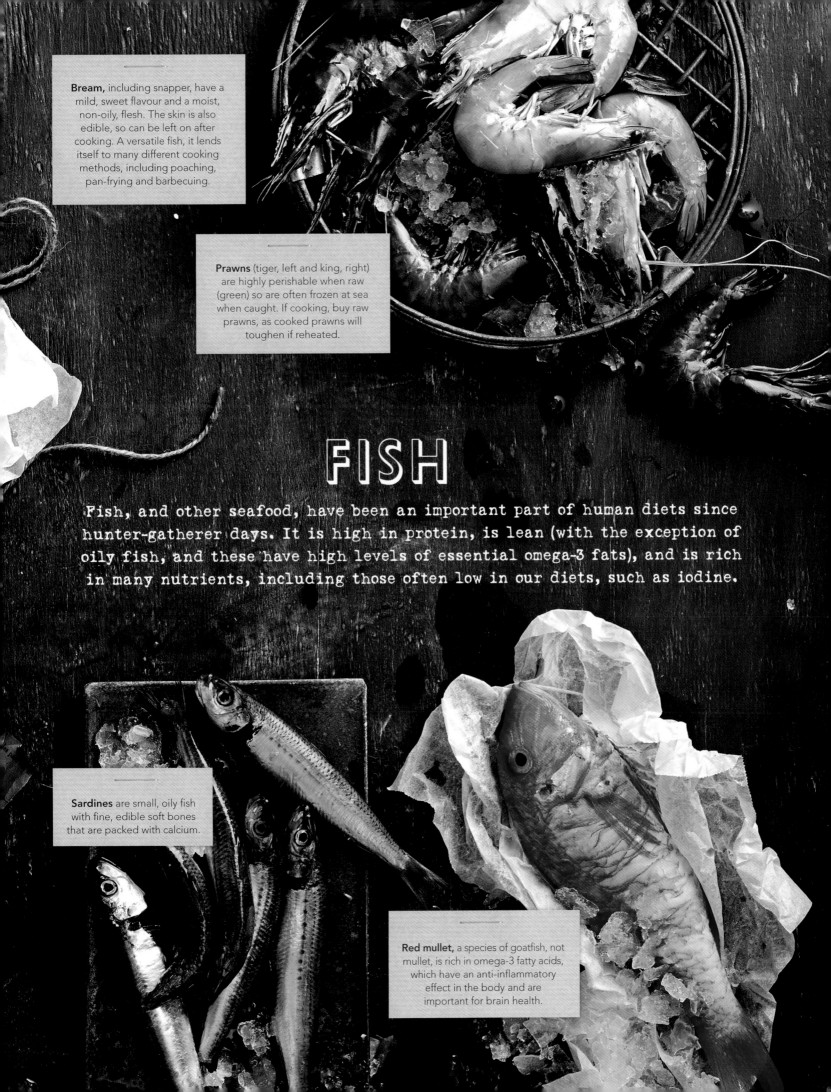

Bream, including snapper, have a mild, sweet flavour and a moist, non-oily, flesh. The skin is also edible, so can be left on after cooking. A versatile fish, it lends itself to many different cooking methods, including poaching, pan-frying and barbecuing.

Prawns (tiger, left and king, right) are highly perishable when raw (green) so are often frozen at sea when caught. If cooking, buy raw prawns, as cooked prawns will toughen if reheated.

FISH

Fish, and other seafood, have been an important part of human diets since hunter-gatherer days. It is high in protein, is lean (with the exception of oily fish, and these have high levels of essential omega-3 fats), and is rich in many nutrients, including those often low in our diets, such as iodine.

Sardines are small, oily fish with fine, edible soft bones that are packed with calcium.

Red mullet, a species of goatfish, not mullet, is rich in omega-3 fatty acids, which have an anti-inflammatory effect in the body and are important for brain health.

moroccan lamb and chickpea wraps

200g (6 ounces) lamb fillets

125g (4 ounces) canned chickpeas (garbanzo beans), rinsed, drained

60g (2 ounces) drained char-grilled capsicum (bell pepper), sliced thinly

½ small red onion (50g), chopped finely

1 large tomato (220g), chopped finely

¼ cup loosely packed fresh mint leaves

2 tablespoons lemon juice

1 teaspoon olive oil

¼ cup (70g) low-fat plain yoghurt

¼ teaspoon harissa paste

6 butter (boston) lettuce leaves

2 rye mountain breads (50g)

1 Cook lamb on a heated oiled grill plate (or grill or barbecue) until cooked as desired. Cover lamb; rest for 5 minutes, then slice thickly.

2 Meanwhile, combine chickpeas, capsicum, onion, tomato, mint, juice and oil in a large bowl; stir to combine.

3 Combine yoghurt and harissa in a small bowl.

4 Divide yoghurt mixture, lettuce, lamb and chickpea mixture between wraps. Roll firmly to enclose filling.

prep + cook time 15 minutes **serves** 2

nutritional count per serving 9.9g total fat (2.6g saturated fat); 1593kJ (381 cal); 34.8g carbohydrate; 33.3g protein; 5.9g fibre; 389mg sodium; low GI

tips There are many types of mountain bread available; choose your favourite for this recipe. Harissa is a very hot chilli paste that varies in strength between brands. Reduce the amount of harissa to suit your taste if you are not used to fiery heat. To take to work, transport the wrap in an airtight container; keep refrigerated.

chermoula tuna, chickpea and broad bean salad

200g (6½-ounce) piece tuna steak

1 cup (150g) frozen broad (fava) beans

150g (4½ ounces) green beans, trimmed, cut into thirds

420g (13½ ounce) canned no-added salt chickpeas (garbanzo beans), rinsed, drained

½ cup firmly packed fresh flat-leaf parsley leaves

1 medium lemon (140g), peeled, segmented

1 tablespoon lemon juice

1 tablespoon olive oil

chermoula

½ small red onion (50g), chopped coarsely

1 clove garlic, peeled

1 cup firmly packed fresh coriander (cilantro), chopped roughly

1 cup firmly packed fresh flat-leaf parsley, chopped coarsely

1 teaspoon each ground cumin and smoked paprika

1 tablespoon olive oil

1 Make chermoula. Reserve three-quarters of the chermoula.

2 Place tuna in a shallow dish with remaining chermoula; toss to coat. Cover, refrigerate for 30 minutes.

3 Meanwhile, place broad beans in a heatproof bowl, cover with boiling water; stand for 2 minutes. Rinse under cold water; drain. Peel beans.

4 Boil, steam or microwave green beans until just tender; drain, rinse under cold water, drain.

5 Cook tuna on a heated oiled grill plate (or grill or barbecue) for 2 minutes each side or until slightly charred on the outside but still rare in the centre; cover, stand for 5 minutes. Cut tuna, across the grain, into thick slices.

6 Combine broad beans, green beans, chickpeas, parsley and lemon segments in a medium bowl with combined juice and oil. Serve tuna with salad; top with reserved chermoula.

chermoula Blend or process ingredients until just combined.

prep + cook time 30 minutes (+ refrigeration) **serves** 2
nutritional count per serving 23.6g total fat (3.7g saturated fat); 2208kJ (527 cal); 29.6g carbohydrate; 43.7g protein; 18.1g fibre; 220mg sodium; medium GI

tips Swap the tuna for salmon. Purchase sashimi-grade tuna for this recipe. If the chermoula ingredients aren't blending well, add 1 tablespoon of water to the mixture.

quinoa salad with char-grilled vegetables and tuna

1 small red capsicum (bell pepper) (150g), quartered

1 medium zucchini (120g), sliced thinly

1 baby eggplant (60g), sliced thinly

1 small red onion (100g), cut into wedges

⅓ cup (70g) quinoa, rinsed, drained

⅔ cup (160ml) water

2 teaspoons olive oil

¼ cup (60ml) lemon juice

1 teaspoon dijon mustard

185g (6½ ounces) canned tuna in springwater, drained

2 tablespoons baby basil leaves

1 Cook capsicum, zucchini, eggplant and onion on a heated oiled grill plate (or grill or barbecue) until tender. Slice capsicum thickly.

2 Meanwhile, place quinoa in a small saucepan with the water; bring to the boil. Reduce heat to low; simmer, covered, for 15 minutes or until tender and water is absorbed. Remove from heat; stand for 10 minutes, then fluff with a fork.

3 Combine oil, juice and mustard in a screw-top jar; shake well.

4 Place quinoa, vegetables and tuna in a bowl with dressing; toss gently to combine. Serve topped with basil leaves.

prep + cook time 25 minutes **serves** 2
nutritional count per serving 9.1g total fat (1.7g saturated fat); 1332kJ (318 cal); 28.9g carbohydrate; 26g protein; 5.8g fibre; 118g sodium; low GI

tips Vegetables can be grilled a day ahead; store, covered, in the fridge. The salad can be served warm or cold; add some rocket (arugula) or spinach leaves, if you like. To take to work, transport in an airtight container; keep refrigerated.

GLUTEN-, DAIRY- AND NUT-FREE

tuna & quinoa tabbouleh rolls

Bring ¼ cup rinsed, drained quinoa and ¾ cup of water to the boil in a small saucepan over high heat. Reduce heat to low; cook, covered, for 15 minutes or until liquid is absorbed. Cool. Transfer quinoa to a small bowl, add 1 finely chopped medium tomato, 1 finely sliced green onion (scallion), 2 tablespoons each of coarsely chopped fresh flat-leaf parsley and mint, 1 tablespoon olive oil and 1½ tablespoons lemon juice; stir to combine. Season to taste. Cut two gluten-free rolls in half; spread half a mashed avocado evenly between roll bases. Divide 95g (3oz) canned drained flaked tuna over avocado and top with 1 tablespoon radish sprouts. Top roll tops with quinoa tabbouleh. Sandwich bread rolls together to serve.

prep + cook time 25 minutes (+ cooling) **serves** 2
nutritional count per serving 19.3g total fat (2.9g saturated fat); 1764kJ (421 cal); 40.7g carbohydrate; 19.3g protein; 4.7g fibre

tip Use poached chicken breast or salmon instead of tuna.

(recipes pictured pages 78-79)

GLUTEN-, DAIRY- AND NUT-FREE

pastrami rolls with silver beet slaw

To make silver beet coleslaw, cut 1 medium carrot into matchsticks; combine in a medium bowl with 2 finely shredded medium silver beet leaves, 1 thinly sliced green onion (scallion), 2 tablespoons plain soy yoghurt and 1½ teaspoons dijon mustard. Season to taste. Cut two gluten-free rolls in half. Spoon silver beet coleslaw equally between roll bases. Top each roll top with 50g (1½oz) pastrami slices. Sandwich bread rolls together to serve.

prep time 15 minutes **serves** 2
nutritional count per serving 3.9g total fat (1g saturated fat); 883kJ (211 cal); 27.3g carbohydrate; 14.3g protein; 4.3g fibre

tips Replace the mustard with gluten-free horseradish for an alternate option. Use roast beef slices instead of the pastrami.

3

VEGAN, GLUTEN-, DAIRY-,
EGG- AND NUT-FREE

char-grilled vegie
& rocket rolls

Drain 280g (9oz) jar of char-grilled vegetables; pat dry on
paper towel, season to taste. Cut two gluten-free rolls in half.
Spread ⅓ cup gluten-free moroccan pumpkin dip evenly over
roll bases; top equally with char-grilled vegetables. Divide 20g
(¾oz) baby rocket leaves between roll tops. Sandwich bread
rolls together to serve.

prep time 15 minutes **serves** 2
nutritional count per serving 20.9g total fat (2.1g saturated fat);
1488kJ (355 cal); 34g carbohydrate; 7.1g protein; 1.8g fibre

tip Leftover pumpkin dip can be eaten with gluten-free crackers.

4

GLUTEN-, DAIRY- AND
NUT-FREE

chicken & avocado
salad rolls

Combine 1 cup sliced cooked chicken, ⅓ cup coarsely chopped
fresh coriander, 2 tablespoons coarsely chopped fresh mint,
2 teaspoons finely grated lemon rind and 1 tablespoon each of
lemon juice and grapeseed oil in a small bowl; season. Cut two
gluten-free rolls in half. Spoon chicken mixture equally over roll
bases. Top roll tops evenly with ½ medium thinly sliced avocado
and 1 each medium lebanese cucumber and carrot sliced into
ribbons. Sandwich bread rolls together to serve.

prep time 20 minutes **serves** 2
nutritional count per serving 27.8g total fat (5.3g saturated fat);
2045kJ (489 cal); 29.2g carbohydrate; 27g protein; 7.4g fibre

tips Use a vegetable peeler to slice ribbons from the carrot
and cucumber. We used skinless barbecue chicken breasts.

1

SANDWICH TOGETHER

SANDWICH TOGETHER

2

3

SANDWICH TOGETHER

4

SANDWICH TOGETHER

indian-spiced patties with carrot raita

420g (13½ ounces) canned no-added salt chickpeas (garbanzo beans), rinsed, drained

1 fresh long green chilli, chopped coarsely

¼ cup firmly packed fresh mint leaves

1½ teaspoons ground cumin

½ teaspoon ground cinnamon

1 clove garlic, crushed

1 teaspoon finely grated fresh ginger

2 tablespoons water

cooking-oil spray

30g (1 ounce) baby spinach leaves

1 wholemeal pitta bread (80g), warmed

2 lemon wedges

carrot raita

½ cup (140g) low-fat plain yoghurt or soy-milk yoghurt

½ teaspoon ground cumin

½ small carrot (35g), grated coarsely

1 Make carrot raita.

2 Blend or process chickpeas, chilli, mint, cumin, cinnamon, garlic, ginger and the water until just smooth. Shape two level tablespoons of mixture into patties.

3 Lightly spray a large non-stick frying pan with oil; cook patties, over medium heat, for 3 minutes each side or until browned and heated through.

4 Serve patties with the spinach, pitta bread, lemon wedges and raita.

carrot raita Combine ingredients in a small bowl.

prep + cook time 30 minutes **serves** 2

nutritional count per serving 6g total fat (0.6g saturated fat); 1545kJ (369 cal); 55.6g carbohydrate; 20g protein; 5.5g fibre; 275mg sodium; low GI

tips Check the consistency of the pattie mixture after processing it by pinching it with your fingers - it should hold together. If not, add an extra 1 tablespoon water. To take to work, transport the patties in a microwaveable container and the spinach and raita in separate airtight containers; keep refrigerated. Reheat patties in a microwave.

POWER
LUNCH

Most fruitarians take the vegan diet a step further and will only eat foods that can be harvested from a plant so long as it is done without harming the plant. This restricts their diet to fruit, honey, nuts, seeds and olive oil. Nutritional deficiencies are likely on such a restrictive diet if followed for too long.

IF YOU'RE HAPPY TO EAT EGGS, THEY ARE AN EXCELLENT WAY TO BOOST YOUR PROTEIN INTAKE. THEY ALSO PROVIDE ELEVEN VITAMINS AND MINERALS INCLUDING VITAMIN B12 (NOT FOUND IN PLANT FOODS), AND A, E & B-GROUP VITAMINS AND IRON. THESE MICRONUTRIENTS ARE ALL FOUND IN THE YOLK, SO BE SURE TO EAT THE WHOLE EGG.

Similar to vegan diets, vegetarian diets have all the benefits from eating generous amounts of plant foods. However, vegetarians who simply cut out meat and don't give any thought as to what to replace it with, or who rely on packaged, processed vegetarian foods, are not eating well. The irony is that despite the title, many vegetarians do not eat enough vegies!

LEGUMES INCLUDING LENTILS, BEANS AND CHICKPEAS, ARE TERRIFIC PLANT SOURCES OF PROTEIN, IRON AND ZINC. THEY'RE ALSO RICH IN FOLATE: THIS B-GROUP VITAMIN PLAYS AN ESSENTIAL ROLE IN PREVENTING DAMAGE TO DNA AND TO CELLS AROUND THE BODY AS WE AGE.

To maximise your intake of nutrients while following a vegetarian diet, consume as many plant foods as possible: include vegies, fruits, legumes, nuts, seeds and wholegrains everyday.

Pescetarian is a type of vegetarian diet that includes fish and other seafood, but no meat or poultry. Pescetarians may or may not eat eggs and/or dairy foods.

PLANT FOODS THAT NATURALLY CONTAIN CALCIUM INCLUDE SESAME SEEDS, TAHINI (SESAME SEED PASTE), SEAWEED, TOFU, ALMONDS, LEAFY GREENS SUCH AS SPINACH, KALE AND WATERCRESS, AND LEGUMES (LENTILS AND BEANS).

Mushrooms are a valuable addition to a vegetarian diet. They have more protein than most vegetables and a serve provides over 20% of the daily needs for each of the B vitamins riboflavin, niacin, pantothenic acid and biotin, and the minerals selenium and copper.

VEGETARIAN

A vegetarian diet, including lacto- and ovo- vegetarians, is easier to follow than a vegan diet, as most vegetarians will consume some animal by-products. Essentially, vegetarians avoid the flesh of any animal, fish or seafood, but will consume animal products where the animal did not have to lose their life. For example ovo-vegetarians will consume eggs, while lacto-vegetarians are happy to include dairy foods. Lacto-ovo vegetarians will consume both and this is therefore the broadest and easiest to follow version of a vegetarian diet.

Nuts, provided you have no allergies of course, provide a wealth of beneficial nutrients to a vegetarian diet. Nuts provide significant protein, lots of fibre and a bundle of nutrients including vitamin E, magnesium, potassium and iron, along with a wealth of antioxidants and healthy fats.

DAIRY FOODS ARE RICH IN HIGH-QUALITY PROTEIN, MEANING ALL OF THE ESSENTIAL AMINO ACIDS NECESSARY FOR THE BODY TO FUNCTION PROPERLY ARE PRESENT. IF YOU'RE NOT CONSUMING DAIRY FOODS, YOU NEED TO INCLUDE OTHER SOURCES OF CALCIUM, SUCH AS SOY MILKS FORTIFIED WITH CALCIUM, IN YOUR DIET.

barley and vegetable soup with crunchy seeds

2 tablespoons extra virgin olive oil

1 large red onion (300g), chopped into small pieces

1 medium parsnip (250g), chopped into small pieces

2 stalks celery (300g), trimmed, chopped into small pieces

4 cloves garlic, chopped finely

1 cup (250ml) bottled tomato pasta sauce (passata)

1 litre (4 cups) vegetable stock

1 litre (4 cups) water

2 medium red capsicums (bell peppers) (400g), chopped into small pieces

400g (12½ ounces) canned cannellini beans, rinsed, drained

½ cup (100g) pearl barley or spelt, rinsed, drained

2 tablespoons pepitas (pumpkin seeds)

2 tablespoons sunflower seeds

2 tablespoons rinsed, drained baby capers

2 tablespoons dried currants

¼ cup loosely packed torn fresh basil leaves

½ cup (40g) finely grated parmesan or soy cheese

1 Heat half the oil in a large saucepan over medium heat; cook onion, parsnip, celery and garlic, stirring, for 5 minutes or until vegetables have softened.

2 Add sauce, stock and the water; bring to the boil. Stir in capsicum, beans and barley; simmer, covered, for 25 minutes or until barley is tender. Season to taste.

3 Meanwhile, heat remaining oil in a small frying pan over medium-high heat; cook seeds and capers, stirring, until browned lightly and fragrant. Add currants; stir until combined.

4 Just before serving, stir basil into soup. Ladle soup into serving bowls; sprinkle with seed mixture and cheese.

prep + cook time 45 minutes **serves** 6
nutritional count per serving 11.1g total fat (2.7g saturated fat); 1244kJ (298 cal); 34.2g carbohydrate; 11.8g protein; 9.2g fibre

tip This soup, without the seed topping, can be frozen for up to 3 months.

vegetable tom yum soup

2 tablespoons vegetable oil

1 teaspoon finely grated fresh ginger

1 clove garlic, crushed

2 x 20cm (8-inch) stalks lemon grass (40g), chopped finely

2 fresh long red chillies, chopped finely

100g (3 ounces) fresh shiitake mushrooms, sliced thickly

125g (4 ounces) cherry tomatoes, halved

2 green onions (scallions), sliced thinly

2 teaspoons finely grated palm sugar or blackstrap molasses (see tips)

¼ cup (60ml) soy sauce or coconut aminos (see tips)

¼ cup (60ml) lime juice

2 cups (160g) bean sprouts

¼ cup loosely packed fresh coriander leaves (cilantro)

stock

1 fresh long red chilli, sliced thinly

2 green onions (scallions), sliced thinly

1 cup loosely packed fresh coriander leaves (cilantro), sliced thinly

1 teaspoon finely grated fresh ginger

6 fresh kaffir lime leaves, torn

2 tablespoons tomato paste

1 tablespoon finely grated lime rind

2 litres (8 cups) water

2 cups (500ml) vegetable stock

1 Make stock.

2 Heat oil in a large saucepan over medium heat; cook ginger, garlic, lemon grass and half the chilli, stirring, for 3 minutes or until fragrant. Add mushrooms; cook, stirring, for 2 minutes.

3 Stir in stock, tomato, onion, sugar and sauce; bring to the boil. Reduce heat; simmer for 5 minutes.

4 Just before serving, stir in juice. Ladle soup into serving bowls; top with combined bean sprouts, coriander and remaining chilli.

stock Place ingredients in a large saucepan; bring to the boil. Reduce heat; simmer, uncovered, for 20 minutes, using a large ladle to skim any scum from the surface of the stock. Remove from heat. Strain stock through a fine sieve into a jug or heatproof bowl; discard solids. You will need 3 litres (12 cups) stock.

prep + cook time 40 minutes **serves** 4

nutritional count per serving 10.3g total fat (1.3g saturated fat); 603kJ (144 cal); 7g carbohydrate; 4.8g protein; 2.9g fibre

tips You will need about 3 limes for this recipe. For paleo, substitute coconut aminos, made from the raw sap of the coconut tree, for soy sauce and molasses for palm sugar. Take to work in an airtight microwavable container; keep refrigerated. Reheat soup in a microwave.

spiced freekeh with cucumber and garlic minted yoghurt

2 tablespoons olive oil

1 large brown onion (200g), chopped finely

2 cloves garlic, crushed

2 medium carrots (240g), diced into small cubes

1 teaspoon ground allspice

1 teaspoon ground coriander

½ teaspoon chilli powder

2 teaspoons cumin seeds

1½ cups (300g) cracked greenwheat freekeh

1 bay leaf

2½ cups (625ml) vegetable stock or water

2 lebanese cucumbers (260g)

1 fresh long green chilli, sliced thinly

½ cup fresh coriander (cilantro) leaves

½ cup (80g) flaked almonds, roasted

garlic minted yoghurt

1½ cups (420g) greek-style yoghurt

2 cloves garlic, crushed

¼ cup lightly packed finely chopped fresh mint

1 Heat oil in a large saucepan over medium heat; cook onion, garlic and carrot, stirring, for 3 minutes. Add spices and seeds; cook, stirring, for 2 minutes. Stir in freekeh to coat. Add bay leaf and stock; bring to the boil. Reduce heat to low; cook, covered, for 20 minutes or until most of the liquid is absorbed. Remove from heat; stand, covered, for 10 minutes.

2 Meanwhile, make garlic minted yoghurt.

3 Using a vegetable peeler, peel cucumbers lengthways into long thin ribbons.

4 Serve freekeh mixture topped with yoghurt, cucumber and combined chilli, coriander and nuts.

garlic minted yoghurt Combine ingredients in a small bowl; season to taste.

prep + cook time 45 minutes **serves** 6

nutritional count per serving 19.4g total fat (4.3g saturated fat); 1886kJ (450 cal); 52g carbohydrate; 14.9g protein; 12.9g fibre

tips You can use 1 teaspoon ground cinnamon instead of the allspice, if you like. Freekeh is roasted green wheat that contains more nutrients than the mature version of the same grain. It has a delicious nutty taste and texture, and is available from major supermarkets and health food stores.

Raspberry vinegar may be either light, made from fresh raspberries steeped in a white wine vinegar; or dark, made from a reduction of red wine vinegar and raspberry juice.

White wine vinegar is made from a blend of white wines.

Coconut vinegar is made from the fermented sap (or nectar) from the blossoms of the coconut palm tree.

Sherry vinegar is a traditional wine vinegar made from the sherry grape grown in the southwest of Spain. It is aged in oak casks, where it develops a rich mellow, sweet-sour flavour.

Apple cider vinegar is touted as being a cure-all for pretty much everything from sore throats to detoxing the body. Unfortunately, there is very little evidence to back up any of these claims, and some have been completely disproven.

Red wine vinegar is based on fermented red wines. They have a more robust flavour than vinegars based on white wines.

VINEGAR

Vinegar is produced as a result of fermentation of a certain food (apples, coconut, berries, etc) by a bacteria or other microorganism. This process converts the sugars in the food to alcohol, and then to vinegar, which literally means 'sour wine'.

The magic of **vinegar** is best expressed when used to create a vinaigrette. It will take a salad from bland to brilliant with just a splash and a gentle toss. Simply remember the all-important ratio of 3 parts oil to 1 part vinegar, and you have the start of a delicious dressing. Next, add any desired flavours that will complement the dish - a squeeze of citrus, a dash of honey, some chopped herbs or minced shallots; the combinations are endless.

Vino cotto is the result of slowly cooking grape must (the freshly pressed grape juice from young dark grapes containing the skins, seeds and stems of the fruit) until it reduces to a thick syrup. It is then aged to develop its rich flavours.

cauliflower 'fried rice'

½ medium (700g) cauliflower, florets coarsely chopped, stems discarded

1½ tablespoons virgin coconut oil

2 free-range eggs, beaten lightly

½ teaspoon chinese five-spice powder

1 large carrot (180g), halved lengthways, sliced thinly on the diagonal

1 medium red onion (170g), cut into thin wedges

300g (9½ ounces) broccolini, halved crossways

¼ cup (60ml) water

2 cloves garlic, crushed

1 tablespoon finely grated fresh ginger

2 green onions (scallions), sliced thinly

2 teaspoons sesame oil

1 fresh long red chilli, sliced thinly

1 Pulse cauliflower in a food processor until cut into rice-sized pieces. Steam or microwave for 6 minutes or until just tender, season to taste.

2 Meanwhile, heat a large wok on high heat; add 1 teaspoon of the oil, swirl wok to coat with oil. Add egg; swirl wok to form a thin omelette. Cook until omelette is just set; transfer to a clean chopping board. Roll tightly; cut into thin strips.

3 Add half the remaining oil to wok; stir-fry cauliflower and five-spice powder for 2 minutes or until browned lightly; transfer to a plate.

4 Heat remaining oil in wok; stir-fry carrot and red onion for 4 minutes or until just tender. Add broccolini and the water; stir-fry for 2 minutes or until just tender. Add garlic, ginger and half the green onion; stir-fry until fragrant. Add cauliflower and sesame oil; stir-fry for 1 minute or until heated through. Season to taste.

5 Serve cauliflower fried rice immediately, topped with omelette strips, chilli and remaining green onion.

prep + cook time 30 minutes **serves** 4
nutritional count per serving 11.6 total fat (7.6g saturated fat); 885kJ (211 cal); 8.1g carbohydrate; 11.6g protein; 10g fibre

tips Other vegetables such as red cabbage and capsicum can be used instead of carrot and broccolini in this recipe, and, if you are not on a paleo diet, peas and beans. Remove the chilli seeds if you prefer a milder heat.

vegetable harira soup

Traditionally, harira is a Moroccan soup of lamb, vegetables and pulses, popularly served to break the fast of Ramadan. Our version omits the meat. You need to start this recipe the day before serving.

1 cup (200g) dried chickpeas (garbanzo beans)

large pinch saffron threads

1 tablespoon water

2kg (4 pounds) ripe tomatoes

2 tablespoons olive oil

2 medium brown onions (340g), chopped coarsely

2 stalks celery (300g), trimmed, chopped coarsely

1½ teaspoons ground cinnamon

1 teaspoon each ground turmeric and ginger

1.25 litres (5 cups) water

1 cup (200g) french-style green lentils

½ cup coarsely chopped fresh flat-leaf parsley

½ cup coarsely chopped fresh coriander (cilantro)

1 Stand chickpeas overnight in a medium bowl of cold water. Drain; rinse well.

2 Soak saffron in a small bowl with the 1 tablespoon water.

3 Cut a shallow cross in the base of tomatoes; place in a large bowl. Cover with boiling water, stand for 30 seconds; drain. Remove skins and discard; puree flesh in a blender.

4 Heat oil in a large saucepan over medium heat; cook onion, celery, ground spices and saffron with soaking liquid, stirring for 5 minutes or until vegetables have softened. Add pureed tomatoes, the water and chickpeas; bring to the boil. Skim off any scum that rises to the surface.

5 Reduce heat to low; simmer, partially covered, for 45 minutes. Add lentils; simmer, partially covered, for a further 45 minutes or until lentils and chickpeas are tender. Season with salt.

6 Stir half the herbs through soup. Divide soup among bowls; serve topped with remaining herbs.

prep + cook time 2 hours (+ standing) **serves** 6
nutritional count per serving 14.1g total fat (2g saturated fat); 1516kJ (362 cal); 28.4g carbohydrate; 23.4g protein; 17.9g fibre
serving suggestion Gluten-free bread rolls.

miso almond vegie patties

2 tablespoons white (shiro) miso

2 tablespoons sesame seeds, roasted

1 cup (160g) almonds, roasted

2 tablespoons vegetable oil

2 green onions (scallions), sliced thinly

180g (5½ ounces) swiss brown mushrooms, chopped coarsely

1 tablespoon light soy sauce

1 teaspoon chinese five-spice powder

2 teaspoons honey

½ cup (35g) panko (japanese) breadcrumbs

1 free-range egg, beaten lightly

2 tablespoons vegetable oil, extra

½ cup (150g) whole-egg mayonnaise

2 teaspoons lime juice

1 lime, cut into wedges

pickled cabbage salad

450g (14½ ounces) red cabbage, shredded finely

2 green onions (scallions), sliced thinly

4 red radishes (140g), sliced thinly

1 tablespoon chopped pickled ginger

2 tablespoons lime juice

2 tablespoons rice wine vinegar

1 tablespoon light soy sauce

1 teaspoon caster (superfine) sugar

1 Make pickled cabbage salad.

2 Process miso, seeds and nuts until roughly combined; leave mixture in processor.

3 Heat oil in a large frying pan over medium heat; cook onion and mushrooms, stirring, for 3 minutes or until browned. Add sauce and five spice; cook for 30 seconds. Add mushroom mixture to processor with honey, breadcrumbs and egg; pulse until well combined but not smooth. Shape 1½ tablespoons of the mixture into 12 patties.

4 Heat half the extra oil in a large frying pan over medium heat; cook patties, in three batches, 2 minutes each side or until golden, adding remaining oil between batches.

5 Combine mayonnaise and juice in a small bowl.

6 Serve patties with pickled cabbage salad, lime mayonnaise and lime wedges.

pickled cabbage salad Place cabbage, onion, radish and ginger in a large bowl. Pour combined juice, vinegar, sauce and sugar over salad; toss gently to combine.

prep + cook time 30 minutes serves 4
nutritional count per serving 59.2g total fat (6.2g saturated fat); 3079kJ (736 cal); 27g carbohydrate; 19.4g protein; 10.6g fibre

tip You can form the mixture into four burger patties then serve with mayonnaise and cabbage salad in wholemeal buns.

soft-boiled egg and brown rice nasi goreng

400g (12½ ounces) gai lan

375g (12 ounces) choy sum

½ cup firmly packed fresh coriander leaves (cilantro)

4 free-range eggs

2 tablespoons vegetable oil

6 shallots (150g), halved, sliced thinly

4cm (1½-inch) piece fresh ginger (20g), cut into matchsticks

2 cloves garlic, crushed

2 fresh long red chillies, sliced thinly

150g (4½ ounces) button mushrooms, quartered

100g (3 ounces) shiitake mushrooms, sliced thinly

115g (3½ ounces) baby corn, halved lengthways

3½ cups (625g) cooked brown rice (see tips)

1 teaspoon sesame oil

2 tablespoons kecap manis

1 Cut stalks from gai lan and choy sum. Cut stalks into 10cm (4-inch) lengths; cut leaves into 10cm (4-inch) pieces. Keep stalks and leaves separated. Chop half the coriander; reserve remaining leaves.

2 Cook eggs in a medium saucepan of boiling water for 5 minutes or until soft-boiled; drain. When cool enough to handle, shell eggs.

3 Meanwhile, heat half the vegetable oil in a wok over medium heat; stir-fry shallots for 8 minutes or until soft and light golden. Add ginger, garlic and half the chilli; stir-fry for 4 minutes or until softened. Transfer mixture to a plate.

4 Heat remaining vegetable oil in wok over medium-high heat; stir-fry mushrooms and corn for 4 minutes or until just tender. Add asian green stalks to wok; stir-fry for 3 minutes. Add asian green leaves, rice, sesame oil, kecap manis, shallot mixture and chopped coriander; stir-fry for 3 minutes or until rice is hot and leaves are wilted. Season to taste.

5 Serve nasi goreng topped with reserved coriander leaves, remaining chilli and eggs.

prep + cook time 45 minutes **serves** 4

nutritional count per serving 18.2g total fat (3.8g saturated fat); 2206kJ (527 cal); 61g carbohydrate; 22.8g protein; 13g fibre

tips You need to cook 1½ cups (300g) brown rice to get the amount of cooked rice needed here. This recipe is packed full of nutrition - mushrooms provide B vitamins and essential minerals; leafy asian greens provide vitamin C, beta-carotene and potassium, and just a few kilojoules. Ginger and chilli are no slouches nutritionally either, both contain powerful antioxidants (which fight the chemical processes that can damage the body's cells).

Pickles are vegetables that have been fermented; this allows them to be stored in jars for many months. Particular bacteria convert the sugars in the food to lactic acid, and this acts as a preservative. Fermented foods promote good gut health and powers our immune systems.

Natural yoghurt is the healthiest option; read the ingredients list to find one with only milk and cultures, and nothing else added.

Sourdough bread is made using a bacterial culture called the 'mother', rather than using yeast to rise the dough. This gives a slight acidity to the bread, which in turn lowers the glycaemic index. The starch present is therefore broken down more slowly and has a gentler effect on blood glucose levels.

Kimchi, traditional to Korea, is a spicy fermented side dish of vegetables, often using cabbage.

White or shiro miso is a combination of fermented rice and soy beans. It's salty, but quite mild in taste.

Miso, Japan's famous bean paste, is made from fermenting soy beans with a particular fungus, salt and other ingredients including rice, beans, barley and other grains. Red miso is fermented from barley and soy beans.

FERMENTED FOODS

Traditional foods were fermented as a means of preservation before refrigeration. And, while they boost the levels of good bacteria in the gut, some are high in salt, so are not suitable for people with kidney or blood pressure problems.

Kefir is a fermented milk drink that tastes a little like yoghurt. The levels of probiotic bacteria are much higher than most commercial yoghurts. For people with lactose-intolerance, kefir is a great dairy option, as the bacteria break down the lactose leaving only a trace in the end product.

Olives picked fresh from the tree are bitter and unpalatable. But for many centuries, countries in the Mediterranean, including Greece and Italy, have picked their olives and fermented them with bacteria and yeast.

Sauerkraut (meaning sour cabbage) is Germany's favourite pickled cabbage; it is low in fat, high in vitamin C and fibre, but also tends to be high in salt.

coconut-roasted pumpkin & cauliflower with chilli lime dressing

Herbs such as basil, mint and coriander add more than just freshness to our plates. Their leaves are rich in flavonoids and surprisingly high sources of vitamins A and C. Coriander is one of the richest herbal sources of vitamin K.

1 small jap pumpkin (1kg), unpeeled, cut into thick wedges

½ large cauliflower (650g), cut into large florets

2 tablespoons virgin coconut oil, melted

⅓ cup (15g) shaved coconut, roasted

⅓ cup (50g) raw cashews, roasted

¼ cup loosely packed fresh coriander (cilantro) leaves

¼ cup loosely packed fresh mint leaves

¼ cup loosely packed fresh thai basil leaves

chilli lime dressing

2 teaspoons lime juice

2 tablespoons fish sauce (see tips)

2 tablespoons brown sugar (see tips)

2 tablespoons peanut oil (see tips)

1 fresh long red chilli, chopped finely

2 tablespoons finely chopped fresh coriander (cilantro)

1 Preheat oven to 220°C/425°F.

2 Place pumpkin and cauliflower on a large oven tray; brush with oil, season. Bake for 30 minutes or until vegetables are brown and tender.

3 Meanwhile, make chilli lime dressing.

4 To serve, arrange pumpkin and cauliflower on a large platter; drizzle with dressing. Sprinkle with coconut, nuts and herbs.

chilli lime dressing Combine ingredients in a small jug.

prep + cook time 50 minutes **serves** 4

nutritional count per serving 27.7g total fat (13.2g saturated fat); 1757kJ (420 cal); 28.7g carbohydrate; 9.5g protein; 11.3g fibre

tips You will need 2 limes for this recipe.
For paleo diets, swap blackstrap molasses for brown sugar, and either avocado oil or macadamia nut oil for the peanut oil.
For paleo, vegans and vegetarians, swap coconut aminos for the fish sauce.

wombok and herb salad with beef and tamarind dressing

1 tablespoon vegetable oil

300g (9½ ounces) beef stir-fry strips

½ small wombok (napa cabbage) (350g), shredded finely

1 fresh long red chilli, sliced thinly

¾ cup (105g) roasted peanuts, chopped coarsely (see tips)

100g (3 ounces) baby spinach leaves

1½ cups loosely packed fresh mint leaves

½ cup loosely packed fresh vietnamese mint leaves

tamarind dressing

1½ tablespoons tamarind puree

½ cup (175g) brown rice syrup (see tips)

2 tablespoons lime juice

2 tablespoons fish sauce (see tips)

1 Make tamarind dressing.

2 Heat oil in a wok over high heat; stir-fry beef for 3 minutes or until cooked through.

3 Place beef in a large bowl with wombok, chilli, peanuts, spinach, herbs and dressing; toss gently to combine.

tamarind dressing Whisk ingredients in a small bowl until combined.

prep + cook time 15 minutes **serves** 4
nutritional count per serving 19g total fat (2.6g saturated fat); 1904kJ (455 cal); 41.3g carbohydrate; 28.3g protein; 7g fibre

tips Brown rice syrup is also known as rice syrup or rice malt. It is available in the health food section in most supermarkets. Use prawns, chicken or tofu instead of the beef.
For paleo, swap cashews for peanuts, 2 tablespoons blackstrap molasses mixed with ⅓ cup (80ml) water for brown rice syrup and coconut aminos for fish sauce.

roast beetroot, garlic and chia seed tart

500g (1 pound) baby beetroot (beets), leaves attached

8 cloves garlic, unpeeled

6 sprigs fresh thyme

2½ tablespoons olive oil

3 medium red onions (510g), sliced thinly

1 clove garlic, crushed, extra

60g (2 ounces) soft goat's cheese, crumbled

2 tablespoons extra virgin olive oil

2 tablespoons orange juice

1 teaspoon white chia seeds

pastry

2 tablespoons white chia seeds

2 tablespoons warm water

1½ cups (240g) wholemeal plain (all-purpose) flour

1 teaspoon sea salt flakes

50g (1½ ounces) cold unsalted butter, chopped

1 free-range egg

¼ cup (60ml) olive oil

1 Trim beetroot, leaving a little of the stems attached. Finely chop enough of the beetroot stems to make up 2 tablespoons; reserve for the pastry. Pick 20g (¾ ounce) small beetroot leaves, cover with damp paper towel; refrigerate until ready to use. Pick a further 100g (3 ounces) of beetroot leaves, shred finely; refrigerate. Discard remaining leaves and stems.

2 Make pastry.

3 Preheat oven to 200°C/400°F. Line an oven tray with foil.

4 Place beetroot, garlic and thyme in the centre of the tray; drizzle with 2 teaspoons of the olive oil. Wrap foil around beetroot. Roast for 20 minutes; check garlic, remove if tender when lightly squeezed. Roast beetroot for a further 10 minutes or until tender; discard thyme. Peel beetroot; cut into quarters.

5 Meanwhile, heat remaining oil in a large frying pan over low heat; cook onions and crushed garlic, stirring occasionally, for 20 minutes or until very soft. Add shredded leaves; stir for about 3 minutes or until wilted. Season to taste. Cool.

6 Roll pastry between sheets of baking paper into a 30cm (12-inch) round. Using a bowl as a guide, trim pastry into a 29cm (11¾-inch) round. Fold in the edge to create a 1cm (½-inch) border.

7 Slide pastry, still on the paper, onto a large oven tray; bake for 12 minutes or until golden. Spread onion mixture on tart base; top with roasted beetroot and garlic, and cheese. Bake for a further 10 minutes or until cheese is golden.

8 Whisk extra virgin olive oil and juice in a small bowl; season to taste. Add reserved small beetroot leaves; toss to coat. Top tart with beetroot leaves; sprinkle with chia seeds.

pastry Combine chia seeds and the water in a medium bowl; stand for 20 minutes. Add flour, salt and butter to bowl; rub together until mixture resembles coarse crumbs. Stir in reserved beetroot stems (from step 1). Whisk egg and oil in a small bowl; add to flour mixture; mix with your hands until just combined. Shape pastry into a disc. Cover; refrigerate for 30 minutes.

prep + cook time 1¼ hours (+ standing & refrigeration)

serves 4

nutritional count per serving 54g total fat (15.2g saturated fat); 3359kJ (802 cal); 54.1g carbohydrate; 17.8g protein; 17.4g fibre

tips You can use a mix of baby golden and red beetroot, or 2 bunches of small beetroot, which you will need to roast for 1¼ hours and cut into wedges. Beetroot stems are tender and sweet, like silver beet, and the slightly sour leaves are also edible.

seeded carrot and cabbage fillo pie

¼ cup (60ml) olive oil

1 small leek (200g), white part only, sliced thinly

2 cloves garlic, crushed

2 teaspoons caraway seeds

2 medium carrots (270g), grated coarsely

250g (8 ounces) savoy cabbage, sliced thinly

¼ cup (40g) dried currants

2 tablespoons finely chopped fresh mint

14 sheets fillo pastry (210g)

⅓ cup (80ml) olive oil, extra

topping

¼ cup (50g) pepitas (pumpkin seeds)

¼ cup (35g) slivered almonds

¼ cup (25g) coarsely chopped walnuts

1 tablespoon poppy seeds

1 tablespoon sesame seeds

herb salad

2 small lebanese cucumbers (260g)

1 cup each loosely packed fresh flat-leaf parsley leaves and curly parsley leaves

½ cup each loosely packed fresh mint leaves and fresh dill sprigs

2 green onions (scallions), sliced thinly

1 tablespoon red wine vinegar

2 tablespoons olive oil

75g (2½ ounces) soft goat's cheese, crumbled

1 Heat oil in a large frying pan over medium heat; cook leek, garlic and seeds, stirring, for 5 minutes. Add carrot; cook, stirring, for 3 minutes. Add cabbage; cook for a further 5 minutes or until vegetables are soft. Stir in currants and mint. Cool.

2 Make topping.

3 Preheat oven to 180°C/350°F.

4 Divide filling into seven portions. Brush one sheet of pastry with a little of the extra oil; top with a second sheet. Keep the remaining pastry sheets covered with a clean, damp tea towel. Place one portion of filling lengthways, in a thin line, along the pastry edge; roll pastry over filling. Starting at the centre of a 24cm (9½-inch) springform pan, carefully form the pastry roll, seam-side down, into a coil.

5 Repeat with remaining pastry, oil and filling, joining each roll to the end of the last one and coiling it around until the base of the pan is covered. Brush the top with any remaining oil.

6 Bake fillo pie for 18 minutes. Sprinkle topping evenly over pie; bake for a further 8 minutes or until golden.

7 Meanwhile, make herb salad. Serve salad with the pie.

topping Combine ingredients in a small bowl.

herb salad Using a vegetable peeler, peel cucumbers into ribbons. Place cucumber in a medium bowl with herbs, onion, vinegar and oil; toss gently to combine. Top with cheese.

prep + cook time 1 hour **serves** 6
nutritional count per serving 30.9g total fat (5.5g saturated fat); 2032kJ (485 cal); 33.8g carbohydrate; 13.5g protein; 10.4g fibre

Green lentil sprouts are related to the famous French lentils du puy; these tiny green-blue lentils have a nutty and earthy flavour. Their hardy texture allows them to be boiled rapidly without disintegrating.

Fenugreek is a crunchy, aromatic sprout with a mild sweet curry flavour. It contains B vitamins, folic acid, calcium, iron and zinc, and many more.

Quinoa and **amaranth** are quite similar seeds. They are fast-growing, high in protein, vitamins A, B, C and E and minerals, such as iron, potassium and calcium.

Sunflower sprouts are similar to alfalfa sprouts; they have a sweet nutty flavour and a crunchy texture.

Yellow mustard sprouts have a delicate mustard flavour and crunchy texture.

Wheat sprouts have a sweet taste. They are quick and easy to grow at home.

Green lentil sprouts are also an excellent source of essential nutrients; they have a mildly peppery flavour.

Tiny **black beluga lentils** have a rich earthy flavour and a soft texture.

Chia seeds have a light nutty taste; they are full of fibre, and are a good source of calcium.

Chickpea sprouts have a nutty flavour and crunchy texture. They are high in protein and carbohydrate, and contain vitamins A, B, C and folic acid, and calcium, iron, magnesium and potassium.

SPROUTS

You can sprout a whole host of seeds like alfalfa, and legumes such as beans and lentils at home. See page 235 for information on growing your own sprouts. Don't forget to soak and cook the sprouts, which makes them safe to eat.

Mung bean sprouts are full of iron, calcium, selenium, zinc and B-group vitamins.

This combination of **alfalfa, radish** and **broccoli sprouts** is high in vitamins, minerals and essential trace elements.

kumara, eggplant and coconut curry

650g (1¼ pounds) finger eggplants

olive-oil spray

2 tablespoons olive oil

1 large brown onion (200g), chopped finely

1 teaspoon finely chopped fresh ginger

1 fresh small red thai (serrano) chilli, chopped finely

2 cloves garlic, crushed

4 cardamom pods, crushed lightly

1 teaspoon each ground cumin, turmeric and garam marsala

800g (1½ pounds) kumara (orange sweet potato), cut into 3cm (1¼-inch) pieces

270ml can coconut milk

400g (12½ ounces) canned diced tomatoes

1 cup (250ml) vegetable stock

2 tablespoons olive oil, extra

1 tablespoon brown mustard seeds

24 fresh curry leaves

400g (12½ ounces) tuscan cabbage (cavolo nero), chopped coarsely

2 tablespoons water

1 Preheat oven to 180°C/350°F. Line two oven trays with baking paper.

2 Quarter eggplants lengthways; place on trays, spray with oil. Bake for 20 minutes or until golden and soft.

3 Heat olive oil in a large saucepan over medium-high heat; cook onion, ginger, chilli and garlic, stirring, for 3 minutes. Reduce heat to low, add cardamom, cumin, turmeric and garam marsala; cook, stirring, for 2 minutes. Increase heat to medium, add kumara; stir to coat in spices.

4 Add coconut milk to pan with tomatoes and stock; bring to the boil. Reduce heat; simmer, covered, for 20 minutes or until kumara is tender. Stir in eggplant; return to the boil. Season to taste.

5 Meanwhile, heat extra oil in a large frying pan over medium-high heat; cook mustard seeds, stirring, for 1 minute or until seeds pop. Add curry leaves; cook for 1 minute. Stir in cabbage and the water; cook, covered, until cabbage is just wilted. Season to taste.

6 Serve curry with cabbage mixture.

prep + cook time 1 hour **serves** 6
nutritional count per serving 23.6g total fat (10.2g saturated fat); 1642kJ (392 cal); 32.7g carbohydrate; 7.9g protein; 10g fibre
serving suggestion Steamed basmati rice and yoghurt.

kale salad with creamy zucchini dressing

Kale, a vegetable rarely featured, is finally in the spotlight. And so it should be: it's a powerhouse of vitamins; tops milk for calcium; and has more iron than meat. Kale has myriad uses cooked or raw.

1 cup (200g) red or white quinoa, rinsed, drained

2 cups (500ml) water

200g (6½ ounces) purple kale, trimmed, washed, sliced thinly

1 large carrot (180g), unpeeled, grated coarsely

1 cup (100g) walnuts, roasted, chopped coarsely

creamy zucchini dressing

2 small zucchini (180g), chopped coarsely

1 large avocado (320g), chopped coarsely

⅓ cup (35g) walnuts, roasted

1 clove garlic, crushed

2 tablespoons white wine vinegar

2 tablespoons walnut oil

2 tablespoons olive oil

1 Make creamy zucchini dressing.

2 Place quinoa and the water in a medium saucepan; bring to the boil. Reduce heat to low; simmer, covered, for 10 minutes or until tender. Drain; cool.

3 Place quinoa in a large bowl with kale, carrot, nuts and dressing; toss gently to combine. Season to taste.

creamy zucchini dressing Process zucchini, avocado, nuts, garlic and vinegar until smooth. With motor operating, gradually both add oils, drop by drop, then in a slow steady stream, until thick and creamy. Season to taste.

prep + cook time 25 minutes **serves** 6
nutritional count per serving 37.8g total fat (4.6g saturated fat); 2041kJ (487 cal); 24.8g carbohydrate; 9.4g protein; 6.6g fibre

tip Quinoa and walnuts are packed with ample protein to make this a meal in itself for vegans and vegetarians, however you could serve it as a side dish with grilled chicken, fish or a poached egg. It would also make a delicious filling for wraps or a sandwich.

serving suggestion Grilled chicken breast and lemon wedges.

vietnamese pancakes with prawns

8 cooked tiger prawns (shrimp) (280g)

½ cup (90g) rice flour

¼ teaspoon turmeric

2 tablespoons reduced-fat coconut milk

²/₃ cup (160ml) water

1 egg

1 tablespoon olive oil

8 butter (boston) lettuce leaves (pulled from the centre of the lettuce)

1 lebanese cucumber (130g), sliced thinly

1 medium carrot (120g), sliced into ribbons

1 cup (80g) bean sprouts

½ bunch fresh mint leaves

½ bunch fresh thai basil leaves

chilli dipping sauce

1 tablespoon warm water

1 tablespoon lemon juice

2 teaspoons low-GI cane sugar (see tips)

½ teaspoon fish sauce (see tips)

½ clove garlic, crushed

1 fresh small red thai (serrano) chilli, chopped finely

1 Make chilli dipping sauce.

2 Shell and devein prawns leaving tails intact.

3 Place rice flour and turmeric in a medium bowl. Add coconut milk, the water and egg; whisk until well combined and batter is smooth.

4 Heat 1 teaspoon of the oil in a large non-stick frying pan (base measurement 23cm/9-inches) over medium heat; pour a quarter of the batter into pan, swirl around base to form a thin pancake. Cook for 2 minutes or until batter has set.

5 Slide pancake onto a serving plate and repeat to make three more pancakes.

6 Serve pancakes with lettuce, prawns, cucumber, carrot, sprouts, herbs and chilli dipping sauce.

chilli dipping sauce Place the water, juice and sugar in a small bowl; stir until sugar has dissolved. Add remaining ingredients; stir to combine.

prep + cook time 30 minutes **serves** 4

nutritional count per serving 14.7g total fat (3.9g saturated fat); 1800kJ (430 cal); 47.1g carbohydrate; 23.5g protein; 6.5g fibre; 449mg sodium; high GI

tips This traditional Vietnamese lunch is eaten by tearing off a piece of pancake and wrapping it inside a lettuce leaf, along with some herbs, sprouts, prawns and vegetables. Slice thin ribbons from the cucumber and carrot using a vegetable peeler. For paleo, swap blackstrap molasses for the sugar and coconut aminos for the fish sauce.

IN
BETWEEN

cherry and walnut smoothie

You need to start the recipe the day before.

½ cup (50g) walnuts

⅓ cup (55g) natural almonds

1¾ cups (430ml) water

750g (1½ pounds) frozen pitted cherries

2 teaspoons pure maple syrup

¼ cup (25g) walnuts, extra, coarsely chopped

1 tablespoon black chia seeds

1 Rub walnuts in a clean tea towel to remove most of the skins. Combine walnuts, almonds and the water in a medium bowl; cover, stand overnight.
2 Blend nut mixture for 2 minutes or until as smooth as possible. Drain the mixture through a muslin or tea-towel lined sieve over a medium jug, twist and press the cloth to extract as much nut milk as possible. Discard remaining solids.
3 Blend nut milk, cherries and syrup until smooth. Divide into 1-cup glasses, top with extra walnuts and chia seeds. Serve smoothie immediately.

prep time 15 minutes (+ standing) **serves** 4
nutritional count per serving 20.5g total fat (1.3g saturated fat); 1422kJ (339 cal); 25.7g carbohydrate; 7.7g protein; 1.2g fibre

tips For a thicker smoothie, blend the chia seeds with the other smoothie ingredients. You can make other flavoured nut milks, using 105g (3½ ounces) total of your favourite nuts and seeds and 1¾ cups (430ml) water.

green smoothie

1 medium lime (90g)

1 medium apple (150g)

1 lebanese cucumber (130g)

½ medium avocado (125g)

320ml (10 ounces) canned coconut water

30g (1 ounce) baby spinach leaves

1 teaspoon finely grated fresh ginger

50g (1½ ounces) baby kale leaves

1 Remove rind with pith from lime; discard. Coarsely chop lime flesh, apple, cucumber and avocado.
2 Blend or process ingredients until smooth. Divide between two glasses; serve immediately.

prep time 10 minutes **serves** 2
nutritional count per serving 9.6g total fat (2.1g saturated fat); 768kJ (183 cal); 18.7g carbohydrate; 2.5g protein; 5.3g fibre

tips Use a variety of green vegetables or fruits, such as lettuce, pear or honeydew melon. For smoothies it is best to use tender baby kale that way you won't need to remove the hard stems. You can top the smoothies with toasted coconut and white or black chia seeds if you like.

apricot & tahini bliss balls

½ cup (100g) dried apricots

¼ cup (30g) linseed meal (flaxseed)

1 cup (160g) almond kernels

¼ green apple (30g), coarsely grated with skin on

1 tablespoon honey, rice malt syrup or pure maple syrup (see tips)

1 tablespoon unhulled tahini (sesame seed paste)

¼ teaspoon orange blossom water, optional

½ cup (40g) shredded coconut

1 Process apricots, linseed, almonds and apple for 1 minute or until mixture is the consistency of breadcrumbs. Add honey, tahini and orange blossom water; process a further minute or until mixture clings together when pressed.
2 Roll tablespoons of the mixture into balls then coat in shredded coconut.

variations

fig and hazelnut Process 1 cup (140g) roasted skinned hazelnuts with 100g (3 ounces) dried figs (remove the hard tops first), ¼ cup (30g) linseed meal, a quarter of a coarsely grated green apple and ¼ teaspoon ground cinnamon for 2 minutes or until mixture starts to clump together. Roll tablespoons of the mixture into balls then coat in 2 tablespoons white chia seeds.

date and cacao nibs Remove and discard pits from 100g (3 ounces) fresh dates; process dates with 1 cup (160g) natural almonds, ¼ cup cacao nibs, ¼ coarsely grated green apple and 2 teaspoons dutch-process cocoa for 2 minutes or until mixture starts to clump together. Roll tablespoons of the mixture into balls then dust with 2 teaspoons dutch-process cocoa.

prep time 20 minutes **makes** 14 balls each
nutritional count per apricot and tahini bliss ball
9.9 total fat (2.2g saturated fat); 573kJ (136 cal); 8.1g carbohydrate; 4.1g protein; 0.5g fibre

tips Wet your hands after rolling every third or fourth ball to prevent the mixture from sticking to your hands. Store in an airtight container in the fridge for up to 5 days or freeze for up to 3 months. For paleo and vegan diets, use pure maple syrup instead of rice malt syrup.

roasted rhubarb and balsamic popsicles

You need a six-hole ½-cup ice-block mould and six ice-block sticks for this recipe.

6 trimmed stalks rhubarb (330g), chopped into 8cm (3¼-inch) lengths

1 vanilla bean, split lengthways, seeds scraped

1 tablespoon balsamic glaze

1 tablespoon honey or pure maple syrup

400ml coconut milk

¼ cup (90g) honey or pure maple syrup, extra

½ cup (80g) natural sliced almonds, chopped coarsely

chocolate coating

½ cup (100g) virgin coconut oil

2 tablespoons cocoa powder

1 teaspoon vanilla extract

2 teaspoons honey or pure maple syrup

1 Preheat oven to 200°C/400°F. Line oven tray with baking paper.
2 Place rhubarb, vanilla bean and seeds on oven tray. Drizzle with balsamic and honey. Roast for 15 minutes or until tender; stand until cool. Discard vanilla bean.
3 Process or blend the rhubarb mixture, coconut milk and extra honey until smooth; pour into ice-block mould. Cover mould with a double layer of plastic wrap (this will help keep the ice-block sticks upright.) Pierce plastic with a small knife, then push an ice-block stick into each hole. Freeze for 4 hours or until frozen.
4 Make chocolate coating when ready to coat frozen popsicles.
5 Line an oven tray with baking paper and place in the freezer. Pour the chocolate coating into a small, deep bowl. Place nuts in another small bowl. Dip popsicle moulds very briefly in boiling water; remove popsicles. Dip the popsicles halfway into the chocolate coating, then dip into nuts. Place on the cold oven tray. Freeze for 5 minutes or until chocolate coating is set.
chocolate coating Place oil, sifted cocoa, extract and honey in a small saucepan over low heat; stir until oil is melted and mixture is combined. Remove from heat; stand at room temperature until cool.

prep + cook time 25 minutes (+ standing & freezing) **makes** 6
nutritional count per popsicle 38.3g total fat (28.2g saturated fat); 1910kJ (456 cal); 23.9g carbohydrate; 5.4g protein; 3.1g fibre

tip If the chocolate coating thickens too much while coating the popsicles, place it in a microwave-safe bowl and heat it on MEDIUM (50%) for 10 seconds to thin slightly. Don't worry if the chocolate coating has a slight whitish look to it, this is simply the coconut fat, but it won't effect the taste.

Green tea is a good source of antioxidants, and studies have shown a reduced risk of several cancers and heart disease with the consumption of green tea.

Maca powder is claimed to help with menstrual problems and chronic fatigue and to act as an aphrodisiac; there is some evidence of the latter, but no evidence for the others. It is a rich source of vitamins C and B6, iron and calcium.

Olive oil is rich in healthy monounsaturated fats and antioxidants. It can help to lower blood pressure, reduce abdominal fat, and lowers the risk of heart disease and some cancers.

Edamame beans are fresh green baby soy beans. Soy is high in protein and is a good source of fibre. It also provides two of the essential fatty acids, and vitamins and minerals.

Pomegranates are rich in vitamin C, fibre and polyphenols, credited in helping the prevention of heart disease and cancer.

Whey protein is a popular supplement in the gym, and evidence has shown that if consumed immediately after a strength-training workout, it leads to better muscle repair than other forms of protein.

Wheatgrass is usually sold as a 'shot' of juice or as a dried powder to add to your own smoothies at home. Unlike wheat, wheatgrass is gluten free. It is certainly nutrient-rich, but no more so than green vegies. A shot of wheatgrass juice will give you a good dose of plant iron and vitamin C to help absorb it.

FOOD TRENDS

The latest trends in food may be more hype than healthy, with many claims not being scientifically substantiated. However, some pack a nutritional punch with loads of vitamins, minerals and fibre.

Goji berries, like most berries, are rich in antioxidants, high in fibre, and stand out for their vitamins A and C, and iron content.

Spirulina is rich in protein and contains all the essential amino acids. It is also a good source of iron, making it a great supplement for vegans and vegetarians.

There is no scientific evidence supporting bee pollen's claim of boosting the immune system. There have been, however, documented cases of severe anaphylactic reactions, see page 234.

salted date caramels

2 cups (310g) fresh dates, pitted

¾ cup (150g) virgin coconut oil

¼ cup (25g) cacao powder

1 teaspoon vanilla extract

2 tablespoons virgin coconut oil, extra, at room temperature

½ teaspoon sea salt flakes

¼ cup (50g) coconut flour

sea salt flakes, extra, for sprinkling

1 Place dates in a medium bowl, cover with boiling water; stand for 10 minutes to soften. Drain dates; discard water.

2 Meanwhile, melt oil in a small saucepan; combine oil and sifted cacao in a small bowl. Stand until thickened slightly.

3 Process dates, extract, extra oil and salt until smooth. Transfer mixture to a small bowl, cover; freeze for 30 minutes or until firm.

4 Line an oven tray with baking paper. Place coconut flour in a small bowl. Using damp hands, roll tablespoonfuls of the date mixture into balls. Roll balls in coconut flour. Using a spoon, dip date balls into cacao coating, then place on tray. Sprinkle with extra salt. Freeze for 10 minutes or until set.

prep + cook time 20 minutes (+ standing & freezing) **makes** 16
nutritional count per ball 12.1g total fat (11.2g saturated fat); 657kJ (157 cal); 12.6g carbohydrate; 1.3g protein; 1.2g fibre

tips Don't worry if the coating on the caramels has a slight whitish look to it, this is simply the coconut fat, but it won't effect the taste. Store and eat the caramels straight from the freezer. Place the caramels in small paper cases to serve.

apricot and cardamom muesli slice

1 cup (150g) dried apricots

2 cups (185g) quinoa flakes

½ cup (70g) quinoa flour

½ cup (75g) sunflower seeds

½ cup (80g) coarsely chopped raw almonds

1 teaspoon ground cardamom

1 teaspoon gluten-free baking powder

1 tablespoon finely grated orange rind

⅓ cup (70g) virgin coconut oil

⅓ cup (115g) honey

3 free-range eggs, beaten lightly

2 teaspoons vanilla extract

2 tablespoons sugar-free apricot jam, melted, strained

1 Preheat oven to 160°C/325°F. Grease a 16cm x 26cm x 4cm (6½-inch x 10½-inch x 1½-inch) slice pan; line with baking paper.

2 Roughly chop half the apricots; place in a large bowl. Cut remaining apricots in half lengthways; set aside.

3 Add quinoa flakes and flour, seeds, nuts, cardamom, baking powder and rind to chopped apricots in bowl; stir to combine.

4 Place oil and honey in a small saucepan over medium heat; bring to the boil, stirring until melted and combined.

5 Add hot mixture to dry ingredients with eggs and extract; mix well to combine. Spread into pan, levelling mixture with the back of a spoon. Top with apricot halves; press down lightly into the mixture.

6 Bake slice for 20 minutes or until golden and a skewer inserted into the centre comes out clean. Brush hot slice with apricot jam; cool in the pan. Cut into slices to serve.

prep + cook time 40 minutes **makes** 18
nutritional count per slice 10.3g total fat (0.7g saturated fat); 839kJ (200 cal); 22.5g carbohydrate; 4.9g protein; 0.8g fibre

tip For a variation, you can use walnuts, pecans, macadamia or cashews instead of almonds.

chewies

2 cups (180g) rolled oats

1 cup (100g) desiccated coconut

½ cup (80g) wholemeal plain (all-purpose) flour

¼ cup (50g) pepitas (pumpkin seeds)

¼ cup (30g) natural flaked almonds

¼ cup (40g) sultanas

¼ cup (30g) goji berries

¼ cup (35g) dried cranberries

1 teaspoon bicarbonate of soda (baking soda)

¼ teaspoon sea salt flakes

⅓ cup (75g) virgin coconut oil

¾ cup (180ml) rice malt syrup

½ teaspoon vanilla extract

1 Preheat oven to 170°C/340°F. Grease a 20cm x 30cm (8-inch x 12-inch) slice pan; line base with baking paper, extending paper 5cm (2-inches) over long sides of pan.
2 Combine dry ingredients in a large bowl.
3 Place oil and syrup in a small saucepan; bring to the boil. Boil until oil is melted. Remove from heat; stir in extract.
4 Add oil mixture to dry mixture; stir thoroughly to combine (the mixture will be quite stiff, use clean hands to combine well, if necessary). Spoon mixture into pan, press down firmly with a spatula or damp hands to level.
5 Bake for 25 minutes or until golden. Turn off oven; leave slice in oven for a further 5 minutes to dry out slightly. Remove from oven; stand slice in pan for 15 minutes.
6 Use the baking paper to help lift the slice onto a wire rack. Cool completely. Remove paper, then cut slice into 16 fingers.

prep + cook time 40 minutes (+ standing) **makes** 16
nutritional count per chewie 12.3g total fat (8.1g saturated fat); 994kJ (237 cal); 27.7g carbohydrate; 3.7g protein; 2.6g fibre

tips Chewies will keep in an airtight container for up to 1 week. If they become sticky, place in a 150°C/300°F oven for 5 minutes; turn the oven off and leave for a further 5 minutes.

chai-spiced popcorn

¼ cup (60ml) olive oil

1 tablespoon powdered stevia or norbu (monk fruit sugar)

2 teaspoons ground cinnamon

1 teaspoon ground ginger

½ teaspoon ground cardamom

½ teaspoon ground allspice

½ teaspoon sea salt flakes

2 tablespoons olive oil, extra

½ cup (120g) popping corn

1 Combine oil, stevia, cinnamon, ginger, cardamom, allspice and salt in a small bowl.

2 Heat the extra oil in a large saucepan over medium heat. Add the popping corn, cover. Cook, shaking the pan occasionally, for 5 minutes, or until the popping stops. Tip into a large bowl.

3 Drizzle popcorn with spice mixture; stir to coat.

prep + cook time 10 minutes **serves** 4

nutritional count per serving 24.2g total fat (3.6g saturated fat); 1328kJ (317 cal); 25.6g carbohydrate; 3g protein; 0.7g fibre

tips If you have one, it's handy to use a saucepan with a glass lid so you can see if all the corn has popped. Popcorn can be made a day ahead; cool and store in an airtight container. Stevia and norbu are both natural sweeteners available from major supermarkets; for further information, see pages 230-231.

raspberry, polenta and pink peppercorn scrolls

2 cups (300g) white spelt flour, plus extra for dusting

½ cup (85g) fine polenta

1½ teaspoons baking powder

pinch salt

½ cup (125ml) buttermilk

¼ cup (85g) rice malt syrup

1 teaspoon pink peppercorns

1 teaspoon vanilla extract

1 tablespoon finely grated orange rind

2 tablespoons rice malt syrup, extra

75g (2½ ounces) fresh raspberries

1 Preheat oven to 180°C/350°F. Grease an oven tray; line with baking paper.

2 Combine flour, polenta, baking powder and salt in a large bowl. Make a well in the centre. Add buttermilk and syrup. Using a butter knife, 'cut' through the mixture until a rough dough forms.

3 Using a mortar and pestle, crush pink peppercorns. Stir in extract, rind and 1 tablespoon of the extra syrup.

4 Turn dough onto a lightly floured surface; knead lightly. Press out into a 18cm x 28cm (7¼-inch x 11¼-inch) rectangle; spread with peppercorn mixture. Using your hands, tear raspberries into small pieces and sprinkle over dough.

5 Starting from one long side, roll up dough to form a log. Cut log into 8 slices. Place slices 5cm (2-inches) apart, cut-side up, on tray. Bake for 25 minutes or until scrolls are risen and light golden. Brush with remaining extra syrup. Serve warm.

prep + cook time 45 minutes **makes** 8

nutritional count per scroll 1.5g total fat (0.4g saturated fat); 1155kJ (276 cal); 58g carbohydrate; 7.2g protein; 1.4g fibre

tips Pink peppercorns are unrelated to black peppercorns, they carry no heat and have a pine-like taste slightly similar to juniper berries. If unavailable don't worry, the recipe will still have plenty of flavour without them. The scrolls are best eaten warm on the day of making. If made earlier in the day, reheat in the oven before serving.

Oat milk has the best protein content of all the grain and nut milks. It provides 6g of protein per 250ml compared to 9g in dairy milk and only 1g in rice milk.

Rice milk enriched with **chickpeas** has a higher protein level than regular rice milk. This milk is produced from brown rice and water, so it's naturally gluten free.

Almond milk, made from water and ground almonds, is a terrific product for vegans and those with allergies or intolerances to dairy and soy. It has about the same kilojoules as skim milk, but far less protein.

Quinoa milk has less than half the carbohydrate content of rice milk. Although the GI has not yet been tested, the lower carbohydrate load will have a smaller effect on blood glucose levels. It is low in kilojoules – lower even than skim milk – but is also low in protein.

Rice milk contains more carbohydrate than cow's milk but not as much calcium or protein.

Hazelnuts are rich in vitamin E, and is a good source of copper, folate and manganese. Hazelnuts are also rich in antioxidants and fibre - especially if you leave the skins on to make the milk.

NUT MILKS

People on dairy-free diets now have myriad milk choices. 'Milks' are made from grains such as oats, rice or quinoa, pretty much any nut, but most popular are almond and soy. There are big nutritional differences between nut milks, so check the ingredient list to ensure you're getting the best quality.

Cashew nut milk is a good source of monounsaturated fats and magnesium, zinc, potassium and iron. It also contains fibre if the milk is not strained.

Soy milk contains a protein content close to dairy milk. However, it can be just as allergenic. Cheaper brands are made with reconstituted soy protein isolate. We recommend avoiding these and choosing one made with whole soy beans instead. Unlike the other milk alternatives, most soy milks are fortified with calcium.

Macadamia nut milk is a delicious creamy milk containing heart-healthy monounsaturated fats and is high in fibre if the milk is not strained.

Rice milk is made from ground brown rice and water, and usually has oil and sweetener in the form of a syrup added. It is low in protein and has a high GI, so while it is not the ideal choice, for those who cannot have dairy or soy it can be a useful alternative.

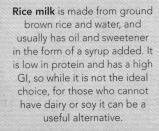

homemade chocolate hazelnut spread

1½ cups (210g) roasted hazelnuts, skins removed

¼ cup (25g) cacao powder

¼ teaspoon sea salt flakes

½ cup (125ml) unsweetened almond milk

⅓ cup (80ml) pure maple syrup

1 tablespoon vanilla extract

1 tablespoon virgin coconut oil

1 Blend ingredients for 5 minutes, scraping down the sides occasionally, until smooth.

2 Spoon spread into a small airtight container. Store in the fridge for up to 1 month.

prep time 10 minutes **makes** 2 cups

nutritional count per tablespoon 30.7g total fat (5.7g saturated fat); 1545kJ (369 cal); 21.4g carbohydrate; 7.8g protein; 4.1g fibre

tips Use as a filling for cakes or cookies, or spread onto bread. To roast and peel your own hazelnuts, spread nuts on an oven tray and roast at 180°C/350°F for 8 minutes or until golden. Rub warm nuts in a clean tea towel to remove skins; cool.

raw turkish delight bark

1 cup (200g) virgin coconut oil

½ cup (50g) cacao powder

pinch sea salt

⅓ cup (115g) rice malt syrup

⅓ cup (50g) coarsely chopped raw almonds

⅓ cup (50g) dried cherries

¼ cup (4g) dried edible rose petals

1 Grease a 20cm x 30cm (8-inch x 12-inch) slice pan; line base and sides with baking paper, extending paper 5cm (2-inches) over long sides of pan.

2 Place the oil, sifted cacao and salt in a medium bowl. Whisk to combine. Gradually add the syrup, whisking to combine.

3 Spread mixture evenly into pan. Scatter with nuts, cherries and rose petals. Refrigerate until set. Break into shards to serve.

prep time 10 minutes (+ refrigeration) **serves** 10
nutritional count per serving 23.3g total fat (19.1g saturated fat); 1126kJ (269 cal); 14g carbohydrate; 2.4g protein; 0.4g fibre

tips Don't worry if the bark has a slight whitish look to it, this is simply the coconut fat, but it won't affect the taste. Because of the low melting point of the coconut oil, the bark should always be stored in the fridge otherwise it will be too soft to handle.

SMART
DINNERS

There is some controversy as to whether a Paleo diet really is optimal, or if it is simply what was available at the time. Most people in that era were killed by infection, so the impact of their diet on the long-term chronic diseases that affect us is not well known.

GROWING IN POPULARITY, THE THEORY BEHIND PALEO DIETS IS THAT AS OUR GENES HAVE NOT CHANGED SIGNIFI CANTLY SINCE THE DAYS OF OUR HUNTER-GATHERER ANCESTORS – PALAEOLITHIC MAN AND HENCE THE NAME – WHAT WE ATE BACK THEN IS A BLUEPRINT FOR OPTIMAL EATING.

It is modern processed foods that are most likely to be high in added refined sugars, harmful trans-fats, too much salt, high doses of refined starch, artificial flavours and colours, and so on.

The paleo theory is that the foods we evolved eating, and ate for many thousands of years, are those best in tune with our bodies. In contrast, modern processed foods and those introduced at the advent of farming some 10,000 years ago, including grains and dairy foods, are causing us harm as our bodies are not designed or equipped to deal with them.

THE MAIN EMPHASIS OF THE DIET IS A FOCUS ON WHOLE FOODS AND RESTRICTING HEAVILY PROCESSED FOODS. THIS IS A PHILOSOPHY MOST NUTRITIONISTS WOULD AGREE WITH.

Bacon, salami, sausages, ham, and other processed meats would not have been part of a true paleo diet.

YOU CAN GET A STEP CLOSER BY CHOOSING TO EAT WILD ANIMALS SUCH AS GAME MEATS (IN AUSTRALIA KANGAROO IS A GOOD EXAMPLE), WILD FISH AND SEAFOOD, ALONG WITH A WIDE VARIETY OF VEGIES, FRUITS, NUTS AND SEEDS.

There are variations of the diet depending on interpretation, with some much stricter than others. For the purposes of this book we define paleo-friendly recipes as having no dairy foods including butter, no grains or products made from grains, no legumes (beans and lentils), no added refined sugars and no seed or vegetable oils.

PALEO

Some argue that as the majority of foods available today, including almost all vegies and fruits, have been changed through agriculture, it is now impossible to truly eat a paleo diet.

Paleo isn't just low carb, high protein eating. In fact, the best estimates of paleo diets show that while our ancestors certainly had a higher protein intake than diets today, they ate a moderate amount of carbohydrate. They also ate about three times more fibre as we recommend today! That means eating generous amounts of vegies, fruits, nuts and seeds alongside meat and fish.

TO EAT A DIET CLOSER TO WHAT OUR PALEO ANCESTORS ATE, DEVELOP AN INTEREST IN NOSE-TO-TAIL DINING. ORGAN MEATS INCLUDING LIVER, KIDNEY AND HEART, WOULD HAVE BEEN CONSUMED ALONG WITH THE BRAIN AND OTHER ANIMAL PARTS WE CONSIDER LESS APPEALING TODAY. THESE ARE NUTRIENT-RICH AND WOULD HAVE BEEN VALUABLE ADDITIONS TO A PALEO DIET.

indian-spiced quinoa cakes with tomatoes

Highly nutritious quinoa has earned its superfood status. It has double the protein of rice and provides all of the essential amino acids – the building blocks of protein.

400g (12½ ounces) kumara (orange sweet potato), peeled, cut into 4cm (1½-inch) cubes

2 cups (500ml) water

1 cup (200g) white quinoa, rinsed, drained

⅓ cup (80ml) olive oil

1 medium brown onion (150g), chopped finely

1 teaspoon finely chopped fresh ginger

2 cloves garlic, crushed

1 fresh long red chilli, chopped finely

1½ tablespoons indian curry powder

⅓ cup coarsely chopped fresh coriander (cilantro)

1 free-range egg

¼ cup (40g) wholemeal plain (all-purpose) flour

1 tablespoon olive oil, extra

500g (1 pound) ripe roma (egg) tomatoes, cut into 6 wedges each

1 tablespoon yellow mustard seeds

2 tablespoons fresh curry leaves

⅔ cup (190g) greek-style yoghurt

2 cups (40g) baby asian salad leaves

1 Cook kumara in a medium saucepan of boiling water for 5 minutes or until tender. Drain well. Mash kumara; you will need 1 cup. Cool.

2 Bring the water to the boil in a small saucepan. Stir in quinoa; cook, covered, over low heat, for 15 minutes or until tender. Drain well. Cool.

3 Heat 1 tablespoon of the oil in a medium frying pan over medium heat; cook onion, stirring, for 8 minutes or until soft. Add garlic, ginger, chilli and curry powder; cook, stirring, over low heat for 3 minutes or until soft and fragrant.

4 Combine mashed kumara, quinoa and onion mixture in a large bowl with coriander, egg and flour; season. Form level ½-cups of mixture into eight 8cm (3¼-inch) patties. Place on a baking-paper-lined tray. Cover; refrigerate for 30 minutes or until chilled.

5 Heat the remaining oil in a large frying pan over medium heat; cook patties, in batches, for 3 minutes each side or until golden and heated through. Drain on paper towel.

6 Heat extra oil in same frying pan over medium heat; cook tomato, mustard seeds and curry leaves, stirring occasionally, for 5 minutes or until tomato is softened. Season to taste.

7 Serve quinoa cakes with tomato, yoghurt and salad leaves.

prep + cook time 50 minutes (+ cooling & refrigeration)
serves 4
nutritional count per serving 31.4g total fat (6.3g saturated fat); 2556kJ (611 cal); 61.5g carbohydrate; 16g protein; 8.9g fibre

spelt pizza with kumara, pepitas and goat's cheese

2 teaspoons (7g) dried yeast

½ teaspoon salt

2 cups (300g) plain (all-purpose) spelt flour

1 cup (250ml) warm water

⅓ cup (80ml) olive oil

3 medium brown onions (600g), halved, sliced thinly

2 cloves garlic, crushed

800g (1½ pounds) kumara (orange sweet potato), sliced thinly

⅓ cup (65g) pepitas (pumpkin seeds)

1 fresh long green chilli, seeded, chopped finely

200g (7 ounces) soft goat's cheese, crumbled

20g (¾ ounce) baby rocket leaves (arugula)

1 Combine yeast, salt and flour in a large bowl; make a well in the centre. Stir in the water and 2 tablespoons of the oil until mixed well. Knead dough on a floured surface for 5 minutes until smooth and elastic. Place dough in an oiled bowl; cover with plastic wrap. Stand for 30 minutes or until doubled in size.

2 Heat remaining oil in a large frying pan over medium-high heat; cook onion and garlic, stirring occasionally, for 5 minutes. Reduce heat to low; cook, stirring occasionally, for 20 minutes or until onion is light golden. Cool.

3 Preheat oven to 220°C/425°F. Oil two 30cm (12-inch) pizza or oven trays.

4 Divide dough in half, roll each half into a 25cm (10-inch) round; place on tray. Spread onion mixture between pizza bases; top with kumara, slightly overlapping the slices, and pepitas.

5 Bake pizzas for 15 minutes, swapping trays halfway through cooking time, or until crust is golden. Serve topped with chilli, cheese and rocket.

prep + cook time 1¾ hours (+ standing) **serves** 4
nutritional count per serving 37.5g total fat (11g saturated fat); 3517kJ (840 cal); 91g carbohydrate; 29.4g protein; 18.5g fibre

tips Use a mandoline or V-slicer to easily cut the kumara into thin slices. For extra protein, add 2 tablespoons chia seeds to the pizza dough.

spanish pork cutlets

1 bunch baby (dutch) carrots, trimmed, peeled

1 medium red capsicum (bell pepper) (200g), chopped coarsely

200g (6½ ounces) brussels sprouts, halved

1 large red onion (300g), cut into wedges

3 cloves garlic, unpeeled

1 teaspoon smoked paprika

2 teaspoons olive oil

1 medium tomato (150g), quartered

2 pork cutlets (470g), trimmed

200g (6½ ounces) green beans or broccoli, trimmed (see tips)

1 tablespoon roasted almond kernels

1 Preheat oven to 220°C/425°F.

2 Combine carrots, capsicum, sprouts, onion and garlic in a large baking dish; sprinkle with paprika and drizzle with half the oil. Toss vegetables to coat. Bake for 40 minutes or until vegetables are golden and tender; add tomato to dish 10 minutes before end of cooking time.

3 Meanwhile, brush pork with remaining oil. Cook pork on a heated grill plate (or grill or barbecue) for 4 minutes each side or until cooked as you like. Remove from heat; cover, rest for 5 minutes.

4 Boil, steam or microwave beans until tender; cover to keep warm.

5 Squeeze garlic from skin. Blend or process garlic, tomato, nuts and half the capsicum until mixture is smooth.

6 Serve pork with roasted vegetables and beans; accompany with roasted tomato and almond sauce.

prep + cook time 1 hour **serves** 2
nutritional count per serving 11.9g total fat (1.9g saturated fat); 1836kJ (439 cal); 25.3g carbohydrate; 46.4g protein 21.2g fibre 224mg sodium; low GI

tips You can use any colour baby carrots; purple, yellow or white, or a mixture of colours. The sauce would also go well with roasted chicken. For paleo diets you may prefer to swap broccoli for green beans.

Habanero chillies

Chipotle chilli

Dried long red chillies

Fresh small red thai and fresh long red and green chillies

The spicy heat of **chillies** comes from the chemical 'capsaicin'. In sufficient quantities this can give a little boost to your metabolism, but that means a whole lot of chilli! It may, however, be more effective as an anti-inflammatory agent and to clear stuffy, blocked sinuses.

Ginger root has a whole host of studied beneficial effects from lowering cholesterol to boosting immunity and easing indigestion and nausea.

Star anise, a hard, star-shaped seed pod of the anise bush, adds a wonderful flavour in Asian cooking.

Saffron has been studied for its potential benefit in relieving premenstrual syndrome and menstrual discomfort.

Nutmeg rapidly loses its flavour, so finely grate the whole seed as you need it.

Turmeric can be bought as the whole root (right), or ground as a bright orange powder. Traditionally used in curries, it's increasingly recognised for its health benefits. It is rich in curcumin, shown to have anti-cancer and anti-inflammatory properties.

Fresh turmeric is said to have anti-inflammatory properties.

SPICES

Traditionally, spices were used to treat digestive disorders, and many are still used for this: ginger remains a popular treatment for nausea and vomiting. Spices are also a rich source of antioxidants.

Ground fennel is more beneficial if crushed from seeds just before using. Commercially ground fennel rapidly loses its potency.

Fennel seeds come from the fennel plant native to the Mediterranean region. The seeds seem to be helpful in relieving indigestion and bloating.

Cinnamon, from the inner bark of a group of trees, has a long history as both a flavouring and for its medicinal value. It is a rich source of antioxidants and has antibacterial and antiviral effects.

tandoori lamb cutlets with green onion roti

12 french-trimmed lamb cutlets (600g)

1 tablespoon tandoori paste

2 lebanese cucumbers (260g)

400g (12½ ounces) red radishes, sliced thinly

1 tablespoon white vinegar

1 tablespoon caster (superfine) sugar

1 cup loosely packed fresh mint leaves

1 cup loosely packed fresh coriander leaves (cilantro)

green onion roti

1 teaspoon cumin seeds

1 green onion (scallion), sliced thinly

1 cup (150g) chickpea (besan) flour

¼ teaspoon xantham gum

2 tablespoons buttermilk

2 tablespoons water

1 tablespoon vegetable oil

chickpea (besan) flour, extra, for dusting

2 tablespoons ghee, melted

1 Combine lamb and paste in a large bowl. Cover, refrigerate for 30 minutes.

2 Meanwhile, make green onion roti.

3 Using a vegetable peeler, cut cucumber lengthways into thin ribbons. Combine cucumber with radish, vinegar and sugar in a medium bowl; toss until sugar dissolves. Stand for 5 minutes to allow vegetables to pickle; drain. Add mint and coriander to bowl; toss to combine.

4 Cook lamb on a heated oiled grill plate (or grill or barbecue) for 2 minutes each side or until cooked as desired. Cover lamb; stand for 5 minutes before serving with cucumber salad and roti.

green onion roti Cook seeds in a small dry frying pan, over medium heat, stirring for 1 minute or until fragrant. Stir seeds, onion, flour and xantham gum in a large bowl to combine; season. Add buttermilk, the water and oil; stir to form a firm dough. Divide dough into eight balls. Lightly flour work surface with extra chickpea flour; using a rolling pin, roll each ball into 2mm (⅛-inch) thick, 12cm (4¾-inch) rounds. Brush a heated small frying pan with ghee; cook roti, over high heat, for 1 minute each side or until lightly golden and cooked through. Transfer to a plate, cover with foil to keep warm. Repeat with remaining roti dough and ghee.

prep + cook time 40 minutes (+ refrigeration) **serves** 4
nutritional count per serving 23.9g total fat (9.2g saturated fat); 1865kJ (446 cal); 28.8g carbohydrate; 25.2g protein; 8.2g fibre
tips Brush roti with garlic oil for a garlic flavour. Roti can be made a day ahead. To reheat, warm in a heated dry frying pan, or wrap roti in foil and place in a heated 180°C/350°F oven for about 10 minutes or until heated through.

broccoli and ocean trout salad

600g (1¼ pounds) broccoli florets

2 tablespoons olive oil

350g (12 ounces) brussels sprouts, halved

3 green onions (scallions), sliced thinly

½ cup (75g) dry-roasted cashews, chopped coarsely

1 tablespoon sesame seeds, toasted

1 medium nashi pear (200g), cored, sliced thinly

200g (7-ounce) skinless, boneless ocean trout fillet

2 tablespoons rice flour, cornflour (cornstarch) or tapioca flour (see tips)

2 tablespoons olive oil, extra

dressing

1 tablespoon sesame oil

1 tablespoon olive oil

¼ cup (60ml) rice wine vinegar

1 clove garlic, crushed

¼ teaspoon cayenne pepper

1 tablespoon gluten-free tamari or fish sauce (see tips)

1 Make dressing.

2 Cook broccoli in a large saucepan of boiling water for 1 minute; drain. Refresh under cold water; drain. Pat broccoli dry with paper towel.

3 Heat 1 tablespoon of the oil in a large frying pan over medium-high heat; cook sprouts, cut-side down, for 2 minutes or until golden. Turn over; cook a further 1 minute or until almost tender. Remove from pan.

4 Heat remaining 1 tablespoon of the oil in same frying pan; cook broccoli for 3 minutes or until browned lightly and warmed.

5 Place sprouts and broccoli in a large bowl with onion, nuts, seeds, pear and dressing; toss gently to combine.

6 Cut trout into 1cm (½-inch) slices. Dust slices in rice flour; shake off excess. Heat the extra oil in same frying pan over high heat; cook trout for 1 minute each side or until golden and cooked through. Drain on paper towel.

7 Serve salad topped with trout slices.

dressing Place ingredients in a screw-top jar; shake well.

prep + cook time 35 minutes **serves** 6
nutritional count per serving 30.1g total fat (5g saturated fat); 1601kJ (382 cal); 9.9g carbohydrate; 14.1g protein; 6.6g fibre

tips Toasting nuts and seeds intensifies their flavour and, if they're a little on the stale side, will freshen them up. Toast the sesame seeds in a dry heavy-based frying pan over medium heat, stirring continuously, for 3 minutes or until they're golden. For paleo, swap the rice flour or cornflour with tapioca flour, which is also gluten-free. You will also need to swap the tamari with fish sauce.

----

spicy roast pumpkin with lamb

¾ cup (150g) cracked wheat

2 tablespoons coarsely chopped fresh flat-leaf parsley

2 tablespoons coarsely chopped fresh thyme

2 tablespoons finely grated lemon rind

2 cloves garlic, crushed

2 tablespoons olive oil

1.4kg (2¾-pound) small jap pumpkin, unpeeled, cut into small wedges

1 cup (280g) greek-style yoghurt

2 teaspoons sumac

6 thyme sprigs, torn

lamb topping

1 tablespoon olive oil

1 medium brown onion (150g), chopped finely

1 teaspoon ground cinnamon

½ teaspoon cayenne pepper

300g (9½ ounces) minced (ground) lamb

1 tablespoon pomegranate molasses

1 Cook cracked wheat in a medium saucepan of boiling water for 10 minutes (it will be not quite cooked). Drain; rinse. Place wheat in a medium bowl; cool for 15 minutes. Stir in chopped herbs, rind, garlic and oil; season to taste.

2 Preheat oven to 180°C/350°F. Line a large oven tray with baking paper.

3 Stand pumpkin wedges, skin-side down, on oven tray; spoon wheat mixture into the hollow of each wedge. Bake, uncovered, for 30 minutes; cover with foil, bake for a further 30 minutes or until pumpkin is tender.

4 Meanwhile, make lamb topping.

5 Spoon lamb topping over pumpkin wedges; serve topped with yoghurt, sumac and thyme sprigs.

lamb topping Heat oil in a frying pan over medium heat; cook onion, cinnamon and cayenne, stirring, for 3 minutes. Increase heat to high, add lamb; cook, stirring occasionally, for 5 minutes or until browned and cooked through. Stir in molasses; season to taste.

prep + cook time 1½ hours (+ cooling) **serves** 6
nutritional count per serving 19.8g total fat (6g saturated fat); 1851kJ (442 cal); 42g carbohydrate; 18.9g protein; 10.3g fibre

----

peanut-free satay chicken skewers

You need 12 bamboo skewers; soak them in water for at least 30 minutes so they don't burn while grilling, or wrap the ends in foil. You also need to cook ⅔ cup of uncooked rice to get the amount of cooked rice needed for this recipe.

⅓ cup (95g) nut-free butter

270ml (8½ ounces) canned coconut milk

2 tablespoons gluten-free tamari

2 tablespoons sweet chilli sauce

2 tablespoons lime juice

2 tablespoons gluten-free tamari, extra

1 teaspoon sweet chilli sauce, extra

12 chicken tenderloins (640g)

200g (6½ ounces) snow peas, trimmed, sliced thickly lengthways

2 cups (300g) cooked jasmine rice

2 tablespoons fresh coriander leaves (cilantro)

1 Heat a small heavy-based saucepan over medium heat; cook nut-free butter and coconut milk, without boiling, stirring until smooth. Stir in tamari, sauce and juice; cook, stirring for about 1 minute or until hot.

2 Combine extra tamari and extra sauce in a small bowl. Thread chicken onto 12 bamboo skewers; season. Cook chicken on a heated, oiled grill pan (or grill or barbecue) for 2 minutes each side or until cooked through, brushing with half the tamari mixture in the final minute of cooking.

3 Meanwhile, boil, steam or microwave snow peas until just tender. Combine snow peas with remaining tamari mixture; toss to coat.

4 Serve chicken on jasmine rice with snow peas and coconut sauce; sprinkle with coriander.

prep + cook time 30 minutes **serves** 4
nutritional count per serving 35g total fat (16.5g saturated fat); 2737kJ (654 cal); 36.8g carbohydrate; 46.1g protein; 2.9g fibre
serving suggestion Stir-fried asian greens.
tips The satay sauce can be made a day ahead; store, in an airtight container, in the fridge. Replace the chicken with beef fillet steak or prawns and thread onto the skewers; marinate overnight in the sauce mixture. Nut-free butter is made from sunflower seeds; it's available in the health-food section of most supermarkets.

baked baby barramundi with pumpkin seed pesto

480g (15½ ounces) asparagus

300g (9½ ounces) green beans or broccolini (see tips)

4 x 340g (11-ounce) plate-size barramundi

2 medium lemons (280g), sliced thinly

¼ cup (60ml) olive oil

pumpkin seed pesto

1 cup (200g) pepitas (pumpkin seeds)

2 cups firmly packed fresh basil leaves

1 clove garlic, crushed

1 tablespoon finely grated lemon rind

¼ cup (60ml) lemon juice

⅓ cup (80ml) olive oil

¼ cup (60ml) water

1 Preheat oven to 220°C/425°F. Line two large oven trays with baking paper.

2 Divide asparagus and beans between trays. Cut three slashes crossways into the thickest part of each fish on both sides; place on vegetables. Top fish with lemon slices, drizzle with olive oil; season.

3 Bake fish and vegetables for 25 minutes or until fish is cooked through (the flesh in the slits will appear opaque).

4 Meanwhile, make pumpkin seed pesto.

5 Divide fish and vegetables among plates; serve with pesto.

pumpkin seed pesto Process pepitas, basil, garlic, rind and juice until well combined. With the motor operating, gradually add combined oil and the water in a thin steady stream; process until smooth.

prep + cook time 40 minutes **serves** 4

nutritional count per serving 57.1g total fat (9.3g saturated fat); 3301kJ (788 cal); 11g carbohydrate; 54.2g protein; 9.5g fibre

tips If you have both trays in the oven at the same time, to ensure even cooking, either swap the trays halfway through cooking time or use the oven's fan-forced function (you will need to reduce the temperature to 200°C/400°F).

You can use four 250g (8-ounce) pieces of salmon fillet instead of the barramundi, if you like. You will need to reduce the cooking time slightly.

For paleo, swap green beans with broccolini.

Chicken breast fillet is good for poaching, or cut into stir-fry strips.

Beef rump steak, a tasty cut from the lower back, is also sold as medallions.

TO-DAYS PRICE 4 (8) PER LB.

Chicken drumstick has darker and more flavourful meat than breast fillet.

Venison backstrap comes from deer. It is lean and tender.

VENISON TENDERLOIN
PRICE/kg $ 89.99 NET WT kg 0.246
TOTAL PRICE

Kangaroo is a very lean cut of meat.

Pork neck roll is cut from the shoulder. It is also known as scotch roast.

Pork loin chop is a tender, tasty and quite lean cut once the fat is removed.

Beef kidneys should be bought fresh. Skin, slice lengthways and remove the tough inner core before cooking.

MEAT

Grass-fed animals and game meats, including venison, crocodile, kangaroo and rabbit, are terrific healthy choices as they tend to be leaner, with lower levels of saturated fats and higher levels of anti-inflammatory omega-3 fats.

Lamb backstrap is a very tender cut. When left on the bone it is known as loin, and is rolled and tied for roasting.

Once cheap, **lamb shanks** now feature prominently on menus at high-end restaurants. When slow-cooked they are deliciously tender.

char-grilled quail with cauliflower and pomegranate salad

Quail is an excellent source of several of the B-group vitamins, especially niacin, with a single quail providing roughly half the daily requirement. Niacin plays a vital role in converting food into energy, and is essential for healthy skin and for maintaining a healthy nervous system.

6 medium quails (1kg), butterflied

1 small cauliflower (1kg), cut into 1.5cm (¾-inch) florets

2 tablespoons olive oil

2 teaspoons ground coriander

1 teaspoon ground cinnamon

1 tablespoon fresh thyme leaves

2 tablespoons pomegranate molasses

2 lebanese cucumbers (260g), diced into small cubes

1 medium red onion (170g), chopped finely

4 green onions (scallions), sliced thinly

1⅓ cups coarsely chopped fresh flat-leaf parsley

½ cup coarsely chopped fresh mint

1 medium pomegranate (320g), seeds removed (see tip)

¼ cup (60ml) lemon juice

¼ cup (60ml) extra virgin olive oil

½ teaspoon honey (optional)

1 Preheat oven to 220°C/425°F.

2 To butterfly quails, cut down both sides of the backbone with a pair of kitchen scissors, poultry shears or a sharp large heavy knife; discard backbone, open quails out flat.

3 Divide cauliflower between two large oven trays; drizzle each tray with 2 teaspoons of the olive oil, season. Bake for 15 minutes or until browned.

4 Place quails on a large oven tray, sprinkle with spices, drizzle with remaining olive oil; season. Place quails, skin-side down, on a heated grill plate (or barbecue); cook, over medium-high heat, for 3 minutes or until browned. Turn over, cook for a further 3 minutes or until browned.

5 Return quails to oven tray; top with thyme, drizzle with half the molasses. Transfer to oven; bake for 8 minutes or until just cooked. Cover quail with foil; stand for 5 minutes.

6 Meanwhile, place cauliflower in a large bowl with cucumber, onions, herbs and half the pomegranate seeds. Whisk juice, extra virgin olive oil and honey in a small bowl. Pour dressing over salad; toss gently to combine.

7 Cut quails in half. Serve quail with cauliflower salad, drizzled with pan juices and remaining pomegranate molasses. Sprinkle with remaining pomegranate seeds.

prep + cook time 1 hour **serves** 4

nutritional count per serving 37.5g total fat (7.8g saturated fat); 2670kJ (645 cal); 23.6g carbohydrate; 47.3g protein; 13.2g fibre

tip To remove seeds from the pomegranate, cut in half and scrape the seeds from the flesh with your fingers while holding the pomegranate upside down in a bowl of cold water; the seeds will sink and the white pith will float.

whiting with pine nuts, currants and tuscan cabbage

¼ cup (60ml) olive oil

1 medium red onion (170g), halved, sliced thinly

1 cup (170g) small red grapes, halved if large

2 tablespoons currants

300g (9½ ounces) tuscan cabbage (cavalo nero), trimmed, chopped coarsely

¼ cup (60ml) red wine vinegar

⅓ cup (50g) pine nuts, toasted

1½ tablespoons olive oil, extra

8 sand whiting fillets (960g)

1 Heat olive oil in a large deep frying pan over medium-high heat; cook onion for 4 minutes or until softened. Add grapes and currants; cook for 1 minute. Add cabbage and vinegar; cook, tossing, for 1 minute or until cabbage is just wilted. Add pine nuts.

2 Heat extra oil in a large frying pan over medium-high heat; cook fish, in two batches, for 1½ minutes each side or until just cooked through.

3 Serve fish on tuscan cabbage mixture.

prep + cook time 25 minutes **serves** 4
nutritional count per serving 30.5g total fat (4.1g saturated fat); 2027kJ (484 cal); 14.4g carbohydrate; 36.2g protein; 4.5g fibre

tip King George whiting is a delicately textured fish with a fine flake and, as is generally the case with small fish, it is a sustainable choice. You can use any other small white-fleshed fish such as snapper, bream, john dory or mirror dory. This agrodolce (sweet and sour) Italian recipe uses currants and grapes for sweetness and vinegar for sourness. This traditional pairing of sour sweet as a sauce or flavouring is thought to have been brought to Sicily by the Arabs.

kitchari

Kitchari, an ancient Indian dish, is often eaten to detoxify the body, and is believed to aid digestion. It is based on the practise of Ayurveda, which focuses on the body's overall balance and harmony.

1 tablespoon olive oil

2 teaspoons finely grated fresh ginger

2 cloves garlic, crushed

3 whole cloves

½ teaspoon cumin seeds

½ fresh long green chilli, sliced finely

1 fresh bay leaf

½ small kumara (orange sweet potato) (125g), peeled, cut into 1cm (½-inch) pieces

¼ cup (30g) frozen peas

½ cup (100g) basmati rice

1½ cups (375ml) water

½ teaspoon salt-reduced vegetable stock powder

½ cup (85g) rinsed, drained canned brown lentils

¼ cup (70g) low-fat plain yoghurt, optional

2 tablespoons fresh coriander leaves (cilantro)

1 Heat oil in a medium saucepan over low heat; cook ginger, garlic, cloves, seeds, chilli and bay leaf, stirring occasionally, for 1 minute or until fragrant.

2 Stir kumara, peas, rice, the water and stock powder into pan. Shake the pan to evenly settle the rice; bring to the boil. Reduce heat; cover, simmer, without stirring, for 15 minutes.

3 Remove from heat; stand, covered, for 10 minutes, then fold through the lentils. Serve rice mixture topped with yoghurt and coriander.

prep + cook time 40 minutes **serves** 2
nutritional count per serving 10g total fat (1.5g saturated fat); 1542kJ (368 cal); 56.8g carbohydrate; 9.7g protein; 4.7g fibre; 375mg sodium; low GI

tip Kitchari can be served as a breakfast dish with a poached egg and wholemeal flatbread.

steak with cashew nam jim and asian greens

800g (1½ pounds) thick-cut beef rump steak

1 tablespoon olive oil

350g (11 ounces) gai lan

270g (8½ ounces) baby buk choy, trimmed, quartered

100g (3 ounces) snow peas or broccolini (see tips)

4 green onions (scallions), sliced thinly

¼ cup (40g) unsalted roasted cashews, chopped coarsely

¼ cup loosely packed fresh coriander (cilantro) sprigs

cashew nam jim

2 shallots (50g), chopped coarsely

2 cloves garlic

3 fresh long green chillies, seeded, chopped coarsely

2 fresh coriander (cilantro) roots, chopped coarsely

½ teaspoon finely grated fresh ginger

2 tablespoons grated dark palm sugar or 1 tablespoon blackstrap molasses (see tips)

⅓ cup (50g) unsalted roasted cashews

⅓ cup (80ml) lime juice, approximately

1 tablespoon fish sauce, approximately (see tips)

1 Make cashew nam jim.

2 Trim fat from steak; rub with oil, season. Cook steak on a heated grill plate (or grill or barbecue) on medium-high heat for 4 minutes each side for medium or until done as desired. Remove steak from heat; cover with foil, rest for 5 minutes.

3 Meanwhile, trim gai lan stalks; cut stalks from leaves. Steam stalks, in a single layer, in a large steamer over a wok or large saucepan of boiling water for 1 minute. Place buk choy on top of gai lan; steam for a further 2 minutes. Add snow peas and gai lan leaves; steam for a further 2 minutes or until vegetables are just tender.

4 Place vegetables on a platter in layers, top with thickly sliced steak; drizzle with any steak juices, then top with cashew nam jim. Sprinkle with onion, nuts and coriander.

cashew nam jim Blend shallots, garlic, chilli, coriander root, ginger, sugar and nuts (or pound with a mortar and pestle) until mixture forms a paste. Transfer to a small bowl; stir in juice and fish sauce to taste.

prep + cook time 40 minutes serves 4
nutritional count per serving 35g total fat (9.7g saturated fat); 2888kJ (670 cal); 14g carbohydrate; 76.4g protein; 7.4g fibre
serving suggestion Steamed jasmine or brown rice.
tips You will need about 3 limes for this recipe. Nam jim can be made a day ahead; keep tightly covered in the fridge until ready to use.
For paleo, swap broccolini for snow peas and 1 tablespoon blackstrap molasses for palm sugar; omit the fish sauce.

seared wasabi salmon and brown rice salad

500g (1 pound) packaged microwave brown basmati rice

350g (11 ounces) sashimi-grade salmon

2 tablespoons sesame seeds

1 tablespoon wasabi powder

2 tablespoons olive oil

100g (3 ounces) baby asian salad leaves

¼ cup (70g) pickled ginger

2 green onions (scallions), sliced thinly

1 fresh long red chilli, sliced thinly

1 large avocado (320g), chopped coarsely

2 tablespoons gluten-free tamari

2 tablespoons lime juice

1 tablespoon olive oil, extra

1 lime, cut into wedges

1 Heat rice following packet instructions; cool slightly.

2 Meanwhile, roll salmon in combined sesame seeds and wasabi powder until coated.

3 Heat oil in a large frying pan over high heat; cook salmon for 1 minute each side or until browned but still raw in the centre. Cool for 5 minutes. Cut into thin slices.

4 Place brown rice in a large bowl with salad leaves, ginger, onion, chilli and avocado; toss gently to combine.

5 Place tamari, juice and extra oil in a screw-top jar; shake well.

6 Arrange rice salad and salmon on a platter, drizzle with dressing; accompany with lime wedges.

prep + cook time 20 minutes **serves** 4

nutritional count per serving 41.6g total fat (8.4g saturated fat); 2893kJ (691 cal); 44.3g carbohydrate; 32g protein; 5.4g fibre

tips If you can't find wasabi powder, use the equivalent amount of wasabi paste and spread it over the salmon before rolling it in the sesame seeds.

Sashimi-grade fish must be impeccably fresh and prepared using extremely strict standards of hygiene as the fish is to be eaten raw. If you are unable to obtain it, or prefer your fish cooked, simply cook the fish for a further 1½ minutes on each side or until cooked through.

sichuan gai lan

Sichuan is a province in southwest China known for its abundant use of chilli and eye-wateringly fiery dishes. For a milder dish, simply halve the sichuan peppercorns, chillies and chilli flakes in this recipe.

470g (15 ounces) broccolini

4 green onions (scallions)

2 teaspoons sichuan peppercorns

¼ cup (60ml) grapeseed oil

1 tablespoon brown rice syrup

4 fresh long red chillies, chopped coarsely

2 teaspoons dried chilli flakes

4 cloves garlic, crushed

400g (12½ ounces) gai lan, cut into thirds

150g (4½ ounces) green beans, trimmed

½ cup (125ml) water

200g (6½ ounces) marinated tofu, sliced

2 tablespoons gluten-free tamari

1 Cut broccolini in half; keep stems and tops separated. Coarsely chop the white part of the onion; thinly slice the green part. Keep white and green parts separated.

2 Dry-fry peppercorns in a wok over medium heat, stirring, for 2 minutes or until fragrant. Grind peppercorns in a small food processor. Add oil, rice syrup, chilli, chilli flakes, garlic and white part of onion; process until chopped finely.

3 Cook chilli mixture in wok over medium-high heat, stirring, for 3 minutes or until fragrant. Add broccolini stems, gai lan, beans and the water; stir-fry for 1 minute. Add broccolini tops, tofu and sauce; stir-fry for 2 minutes or until tofu is heated through and vegetables are just tender.

4 Serve stir-fry sprinkled with green part of onion.

prep + cook time 15 minutes **serves** 4
nutritional count per serving 18g total fat (2.7g saturated fat); 1190kJ (284 cal); 9g carbohydrate; 15.6g protein; 13g fibre

tips You will need 2 bunches of broccolini for this recipe. Substitute any of the vegetables in this recipe with another asian green. Tofu can be substituted with barbecued chicken or smoked chicken breast.

rosemary and tomato barley risotto

1 tablespoon olive oil

1 small brown onion (80g), chopped finely

2 cloves garlic, crushed

1 medium red capsicum (bell pepper) (200g), sliced thinly

1 tablespoon fresh rosemary, chopped finely

1½ cups (300g) pearl barley

1.25 litres (5 cups) vegetable stock

400g (12½ ounces) canned diced tomatoes

1 cup (280g) bottled tomato passata

2 teaspoons caster (superfine) sugar

2 teaspoons finely grated lemon rind

200g (6½ ounces) buffalo mozzarella, torn

1 tablespoon chilli-infused olive oil

½ cup loosely packed fresh flat-leaf parsley leaves

1 Heat olive oil in a large saucepan over medium heat; cook onion, garlic, capsicum and rosemary for 5 minutes or until tender.
2 Add barley; cook, stirring, for 1 minute. Add stock, tomatoes, passata, sugar and rind; bring to the boil. Reduce heat to low; cook, stirring occasionally, for 45 minutes or until barley is tender. Season to taste.
3 Spoon risotto into bowls; top with mozzarella, drizzle with chilli oil and sprinkle with parsley.

prep + cook time 55 minutes **serves** 4
nutritional count per serving 24.5g total fat (9.2g saturated fat); 2476kJ (592 cal); 61.6g carbohydrate; 24.8g protein; 13.7g fibre

tips You could use large balls of fresh cow's milk mozzarella, which are known as 'fior di latte', literally meaning 'flower of the milk', if you like. Use a pinch of chilli flakes or a little chopped fresh chilli and extra virgin olive oil instead of the chilli-infused oil. Passata is pureed and sieved Italian tomatoes and is available from supermarkets.

coconut, coriander chicken and vegetable curry

3 fresh long green chillies

1 large brown onion (200g), chopped

1 teaspoon finely grated fresh ginger

4 cloves garlic, chopped

1 tablespoon ground coriander

1 tablespoon ground cumin

1 teaspoon sea salt flakes

1kg (2 pounds) chicken thigh fillets

270ml (9 fluid ounces) canned coconut milk

2 cups (500ml) chicken stock

600g (1¼ pounds) kumara (orange sweet potato), unpeeled, cut into 2.5cm (1-inch) pieces

300g (9½ ounces) cauliflower, chopped

90g (3 ounces) baby spinach

1 tablespoon sesame seeds

⅓ cup (50g) roasted salted cashews

1 cup (280g) greek-style yoghurt or coconut cream

½ cup coarsely chopped coriander (cilantro) leaves

¼ cup coarsely chopped fresh mint leaves

1 fresh long green chilli, chopped, extra

¼ cup lightly packed fresh coriander sprigs (cilantro), extra

1 lime, cut into wedges

1 Remove seeds from two of the chillies; chop all the chillies (keep the seeded chilli separate).

2 To make curry paste, blend seeded chillies, onion, ginger, garlic, spices and salt until smooth.

3 Trim fat from chicken; cut chicken into 4cm (1½-inch) pieces. Heat 2 tablespoons of the coconut milk in a large saucepan over medium heat, add curry paste; cook, stirring, for 3 minutes or until fragrant. Add chicken; cook, stirring, for 2 minutes or until combined. Add stock and remaining coconut milk; bring to the boil. Reduce heat; simmer, covered, for 10 minutes.

4 Add kumara to curry; simmer, covered, for 5 minutes. Add cauliflower; simmer, covered, a further 5 minutes or until kumara and cauliflower are just tender. Stir in spinach until wilted.

5 Meanwhile, dry-fry seeds and nuts until browned lightly. Remove from pan; cool. Blend nut mixture until ground finely. Stir nut mixture into curry; stir in ¾ cup of the yoghurt and the chopped herbs. Season to taste.

6 Serve curry drizzled with remaining yoghurt, topped with the remaining chilli and extra coriander. Serve with lime wedges.

prep + cook time 50 minutes **serves** 6

nutritional count per serving 49g total fat (20g saturated fat); 3014kJ (720 cal); 30.8g carbohydrate; 36.2g protein; 7.4g fibre

tip Long chillies are usually mild, but can vary in their heat intensity. Adjust the amount of chillies you use (or remove the seeds and membranes from all of them), according to your heat tolerance level.

For paleo, use coconut cream instead of yoghurt and serve the curry without rice.

serving suggestion Steamed basmati or brown rice.

Kale is rich in the carotenoids lutein and zeaxanthin (which have shown to reduce the risk of age-related macular degeneration and cataracts), and is a good source of vitamins A, C and K, and calcium.

Sugar snap peas look just like peas, but are smaller, more tender and have an edible pod with sweet, juicy seeds (immature peas).

Cavolo nero, also known as tuscan cabbage, has good levels of vitamins A, C and K, folate and fibre. It doesn't lose its volume like silver beet or spinach when cooked, but may need longer cooking.

Buk choy (mature and baby) is part of the brassica family. Collectively, these reduce the risk of stomach, colon and lung cancers. It is rich in vitamins A and C and several B-group vitamins, and has small but significant amounts of iron and calcium.

Broccolini is a cross between broccoli and gai lan. You can eat the whole vegetable from stalk to floret. Like broccoli, it's rich in antioxidants that help fight oxidative damage that causes disease and aging.

Green beans are a good source of vitamins and minerals. Firm vegies have more fibre than leafy greens.

LEAFY GREENS

"Eat your greens" were actually wise words of wisdom from our mothers, but there were times when even the threat of no dessert, wasn't enough to get us to eat up. Now we know better... their multitude of protective functions against disease and aging make them powerhouses of health.

Brussels sprouts are in the same family as broccoli and have many of the same benefits, particularly in reducing the risk of cancers of the bowel.

Green peas are one of the best vegetable sources of fibre. They also have a good amount of protein, iron, zinc, folate and vitamin C. Green peas have a high sugar content, but this starts to deteriorate soon after picking.

thai prawns with soba noodles and asparagus

200g (6½ ounces) green tea soba noodles

340g (11 ounces) thin asparagus, halved crossways

½ cup (80g) shelled frozen edamame (soya beans), thawed

1 cup loosely packed fresh mint leaves

1 cup loosely packed fresh thai basil leaves

16 uncooked large prawns (shrimp) (1.2kg), peeled, deveined, with tails intact

2 tablespoons olive oil

2 limes, cut into wedges

dressing

2 tablespoons finely grated palm sugar

⅓ cup (80ml) lime juice

¼ cup (60ml) fish sauce

2 fresh small red thai (serrano) chillies, seeded, chopped finely

¼ cup (60ml) peanut oil

1 Make dressing.

2 Cook noodles in a saucepan of boiling water for 2 minutes or until almost tender. Add asparagus; cook a further 2 minutes or until noodles and asparagus are just tender. Drain, refresh under cold water; drain.

3 Place noodles and asparagus in a large bowl with edamame, herbs and dressing; toss gently to combine.

4 Combine prawns and oil in a medium bowl. Cook prawns on a heated grill plate (or grill or barbecue) for 1½ minutes each side or until just cooked through.

5 Serve noodle salad topped with prawns; accompany with lime wedges.

dressing Whisk ingredients in a small bowl until sugar dissolves.

prep + cook time 25 minutes **serves** 4

nutritional count per serving 25.3g total fat (4.5g saturated fat); 2015kJ (481 cal); 22.1g carbohydrate; 22g protein; 6g fibre

tips Asparagus spears vary in thickness; if the ends are really thick, peel them from the bottom up to within 5cm (2-inches) of the tips. Soba noodles are a low-GI noodle, originating in Japan, made from a mixture of buckwheat and wheat, making them high in fibre and protein. The sodium content is high, however, this is reduced significantly after cooking.

za'atar spiced chickpea salad with fetta and mint

400g (12½ ounces) butternut pumpkin, unpeeled

1 large red onion (300g), cut into thin wedges

1 medium red capsicum (bell pepper) (200g), sliced thickly

1 medium yellow capsicum (bell pepper) (200g), sliced thickly

400g (12½ ounces) baby (dutch) carrots, trimmed

2 tablespoons olive oil

400g (12½ ounces) canned chickpeas (garbanzo beans), rinsed, drained

2 tablespoons za'atar

¼ cup (60ml) red wine vinegar

¼ cup (60ml) olive oil, extra

100g (3 ounces) fetta, crumbled

⅓ cup loosely packed small fresh mint leaves

1 Preheat oven to 220°C/425°F.

2 Cut unpeeled pumpkin into thin wedges; halve crossways. Place pumpkin, onion, capsicum and carrot, in a single layer, on a baking-paper-lined large oven tray; drizzle with half the oil, season. Bake for 25 minutes or until tender.

3 Meanwhile, place chickpeas on another baking-paper-lined oven tray. Drizzle with remaining oil, sprinkle with za'atar; toss gently to coat. Bake for 25 minutes or until golden and crisp.

4 Whisk vinegar and extra oil in a small bowl; season to taste.

5 Place vegetables and chickpeas on a serving platter; drizzle with vinegar mixture, top with fetta and mint.

prep + cook time 40 minutes **serves** 4

nutritional count per serving 31g total fat (7.6g saturated fat); 1967kJ (470 cal); 28.9g carbohydrate; 13.1g protein; 13.6g fibre

tip It is important to have the vegetables in a single layer so they roast quickly without steaming. If necessary, divide the vegetables between two trays.

spinach and broccolini pasta with rocket and walnut pesto

400g (12½ ounces) wholemeal spaghetti

470g (15 ounces) broccolini, trimmed, cut into 4cm (1½-inch) lengths

2 tablespoons olive oil

2 cloves garlic, crushed

400g (12½ ounces) baby spinach leaves

1 cup (240g) fresh firm ricotta, crumbled

½ cup (50g) walnuts, roasted, chopped coarsely

rocket and walnut pesto

60g (2 ounces) rocket (arugula)

1 cup firmly packed fresh basil leaves

½ cup (50g) walnuts, roasted

2 cloves garlic, crushed

1 teaspoon finely grated lemon rind

⅓ cup (25g) finely grated parmesan

½ cup (125ml) extra virgin olive oil

1 Make rocket and walnut pesto.

2 Cook pasta in a large saucepan of boiling water for 10 minutes or until almost tender, adding broccolini in the last 2 minutes of cooking time. Drain well, reserving ½ cup of cooking liquid.

3 Meanwhile, heat oil in a large saucepan over medium heat; cook garlic and spinach, stirring occasionally, for 2 minutes or until just wilted, season. Add pasta, broccolini, pesto and enough reserved cooking liquid to help combine the sauce.

4 Serve pasta topped with ricotta and nuts.

rocket and walnut pesto Process rocket, basil, nuts, garlic, rind, cheese and 1 tablespoon of the oil until chopped roughly. With motor operating, add remaining oil in a thin, steady stream until mixture is smooth. Season to taste.

prep + cook time 35 minutes **serves** 6
nutritional count per serving 42.4g total fat (7.8g saturated fat); 2822kJ (674 cal); 49.5g carbohydrate; 20.7g protein; 6.8g fibre

tip It's a good idea to remove the thin paper skins from the walnuts after roasting as they can add a slight bitterness to the pesto. While the nuts are still warm, rub them together in a clean tea towel to remove most of the skins.
While walnuts and other tree nuts are fairly high in calories, they offer a large array of antioxidant and anti-inflammatory nutrients, as well as valuable monounsaturated and hard-to-source omega-3 fatty acids. If you like, you can use almonds instead of the walnuts in the pesto.

HEALTHY SWEET FIXES

Honey and maple syrup are also sugars, although they are not refined as most other sugars are. In fact honey has been a part of human diets since hunter-gatherer days. But, they are sugars, and so for a truly sugar-free diet you'll need to give them a miss.

NATURAL ALTERNATIVES TO SUCROSE INCLUDE SORBITOL (COMMONLY USED IN SUGAR-FREE GUMS AND MINTS), XYLITOL, STEVIA OR MONK FRUIT (SOLD AS NORBU). THESE ARE ALL NATURALLY SWEET, PROVIDE FEWER KILOJOULES, DO NOT RAISE BLOOD SUGAR LEVELS AND ARE TOOTH FRIENDLY.

The one word of caution however, is that you don't become so fixated with sugar that you forget to step back and look at your total diet. There are many aspects of diet that are important, and blaming just one thing is dangerous as it blinds us to other, just as important, aspects.

Sugar is being blamed for all manner of our ills at the moment. There is no doubt that many people are consuming way too much, and certainly sugar is added to many foods and drinks, even where you would least expect it, making it all too easy for levels to sneak up on you.

Fructose is at the centre of the sugar debate. There is a worrying trend that products and recipes that claim to be fructose-free, simply contain other sugars. These can have a higher GI and have a far greater effect on blood sugar levels than those containing fructose.

ALL CARBOHYDRATES ARE VARIOUS COMBINATIONS OF THE SIMPLEST SUGARS (MONO-SACCHARIDES), WHICH INCLUDE GLUCOSE, FRUCTOSE AND GALACTOSE.

There is a big difference between eating whole foods, such as fruits, that naturally contain sugars, and foods that have high levels of added refined sugars. Whole foods are also rich in fibre and contain a whole host of vitamins, minerals and phytonutrients that benefit our health. They are worthy of a place in our diet.

SUGAR COMES IN MANY GUISES. WHEN YOU READ THE INGREDIENTS LIST OF A FOOD PRODUCT LOOK FOR SYRUPS INCLUDING BROWN RICE SYRUP, MALTOSE, MOLASSES, CANE JUICE, COCONUT SUGAR, MALTODEXTRIN, RASPADURA, AGAVE SYRUP AND TREACLE.

SUGAR FREE

WE LABEL OUR RECIPES AS SUGAR-FREE WHERE THEY ARE FREE FROM ADDED REFINED SUGARS, INCLUDING SUCROSE (TABLE SUGAR) AND SYRUPS. HOWEVER, SUGARS NATURALLY PRESENT IN WHOLE FOODS MAY BE INCLUDED IN A SUGAR-FREE RECIPE.

Simple sugars can be joined in pairs to form disaccharides, such as sucrose, or table sugar (glucose and fructose) and lactose (glucose and galactose) the sugar in milk.

Focus on reducing or, if you like, completely cutting out foods with added refined sugars. Foods with little or no nutritional value, with high levels of refined sugars, should be the first to go. These include lollies, confectionary, biscuits, cakes and sugar-sweetened soft drinks.

rosemary, labne and orange tart

You need to start the recipe the day before.

800g (1½ pounds) greek-style yoghurt

3 free-range eggs

2 tablespoons honey

1 teaspoon vanilla extract

2 teaspoons finely chopped fresh rosemary leaves

2 cups (500ml) clear no-added-sugar apple juice

1 sprig fresh rosemary, extra

3 small oranges (540g), sliced thinly

amaranth pastry

1½ cups (225g) fine amaranth flour

2 tablespoons arrowroot starch

pinch salt

⅓ cup (70g) virgin coconut oil

½ cup (125ml) ice-cold water

1 To make labne, line a medium sieve with a piece of muslin (or a clean loosely-woven cotton cloth); place sieve over a large bowl. Spoon yoghurt into muslin, cover bowl and sieve with plastic wrap; refrigerate overnight.

2 Make amaranth pastry.

3 Grease an 11cm x 34cm (4½-inch x 14-inch) rectangular loose-based fluted tart pan. Roll pastry between sheets of baking paper until 3mm (⅛ inch) thick. Lift pastry into pan, press into base and sides; trim excess pastry. Prick base all over with a fork. Cover, refrigerate for 30 minutes.

4 Preheat oven to 200°C/400°F.

5 Place tart pan on an oven tray; line with baking paper, fill with dried beans or rice. Bake for 15 minutes. Remove paper and beans; bake a further 5 minutes or until browned lightly. Cool.

6 Reduce oven temperature to 140°C/280°F.

7 Drain labne; whisk in a large bowl with eggs, honey, extract and chopped rosemary. Spoon into cooled pastry case. Bake for 25 minutes or until just set. Cool to room temperature. Refrigerate until cold.

8 Meanwhile, place apple juice and extra rosemary in a medium saucepan; bring to the boil over medium heat. Add orange slices to pan, reduce heat to low; simmer for 15 minutes or until tender; cool. Just before serving, drain orange slices and arrange over the cooled tart.

amaranth pastry Process flour, starch, salt and oil until combined. With the motor operating, gradually add the iced water in a thin steady stream until a dough forms. Flatten pastry into a disc, wrap in plastic wrap; refrigerate for 30 minutes.

prep + cook time 1½ hours (+ refrigeration & cooling) **serves** 8
nutritional count per serving 18.4g total fat (13g saturated fat); 1719kJ (410 cal); 49.3g carbohydrate; 11.4g protein; 5.4g fibre

tip If you like, make the whole tart a day ahead and store in the fridge. Top with the oranges just before serving.

salted coconut and passionfruit semifreddo

2 cups (500ml) coconut cream (see tips)

6 free-range eggs, separated

⅓ cup (115g) honey or pure maple syrup (see tips)

2 teaspoons vanilla extract

½ cup (50g) coconut milk powder

1 teaspoon sea salt flakes

⅓ cup (80ml) fresh passionfruit pulp

½ cup (25g) unsweetened coconut flakes

¼ cup (60ml) fresh passionfruit pulp, extra

1 tablespoon micro mint or small mint leaves

1 Pour coconut cream into a medium metal bowl; place in the freezer for 30 minutes or until chilled.

2 Grease a 20cm x 11.5cm x 9cm (8-inch x 4¾-inch x 3¾-inch) loaf pan. Line with baking paper, extending paper 5cm (2-inches) over sides of pan.

3 Beat egg yolks, 2 tablespoons of the honey and extract in a small bowl with an electric mixer on high for 5 minutes or until thick and pale. Transfer to a large bowl.

4 Beat egg whites in a clean small bowl with an electric mixer until soft peaks form. Gradually add the remaining honey; beat until thick and glossy.

5 Whisk chilled coconut cream, coconut milk powder and salt in a medium bowl until slightly thickened. Gently fold egg whites and coconut cream mixture into egg yolk mixture.

6 Pour into prepared pan; freeze for 1 hour or until mixture has thickened slightly. Swirl through passionfruit pulp; freeze for at least 3 hours or overnight.

7 Stand semifreddo at room temperature for 5 minutes before inverting onto a platter. Top with coconut flakes, extra passionfruit and mint to serve.

prep + cook time 30 minutes (+ freezing) **serves** 10
nutritional count per serving 17.7g total fat (14.1g saturated fat); 988kJ (236 cal); 13.5g carbohydrate; 5.6g protein; 2.5g fibre

tips Use a brand of coconut cream that states it is 100% natural on the label. Coconut cream that has 'emulsifying agents' added (it will state this on the label) may cause the semifreddo to separate into creamy and watery layers. For vegan diets use maple syrup. You will need about 9 passionfruit to get the amount of pulp required. You could also peel the flesh of fresh coconut with a vegetable peeler, if preferred and substitute it for the coconut flakes.

ginger, pear and pistachio crumbles

6 medium firm pears (1.4kg), peeled, chopped coarsely

125g (4 ounces) fresh or frozen raspberries

2 tablespoons cornflour (cornstarch) or arrowroot (see tips)

1 tablespoon finely grated fresh ginger

¼ cup (60ml) pure maple syrup

1 tablespoon lemon juice

1 teaspoon vanilla extract

1 cup (140g) pistachios

1 cup (120g) pecans

1 cup (90g) rolled oats

¼ cup (60ml) olive oil

¼ cup (60ml) pure maple syrup, extra

1 teaspoon vanilla extract, extra

2 tablespoons freeze-dried or fresh pomegranate seeds

2 cups (560g) thick no-sugar-added vanilla yoghurt (see tips)

1 Preheat oven to 160°C/325°F.

2 Place pears, raspberries, cornflour, ginger, syrup, juice and extract in a large bowl; toss to coat fruit in mixture. Divide mixture among 6 x 1-cup (250ml) ovenproof dishes.

3 Process nuts until chopped roughly. Transfer to a medium bowl, stir in oats, oil and extra syrup and extract; spoon over fruit mixture.

4 Bake, uncovered, for 1 hour. Cover with foil; bake a further 15 minutes or until crumble topping is golden and pears are soft.

5 To serve, sprinkle pomegranate seeds over the top and accompany with yoghurt.

prep + cook time 1½ hours **serves** 6
nutritional count per serving 42.3g total fat (7.5g saturated fat); 3130kJ (7447 cal); 73.6g carbohydrate; 13.9g protein; 8g fibre

tips If you can't find sugar-free vanilla yoghurt you can stir vanilla extract through greek-style yoghurt. Freeze dried pomegranate seeds are available from health food stores or substitute with unsweetened cranberries for extra antioxidants. For vegan and paleo diets use coconut milk yoghurt. For paleo, substitute arrowroot for cornflour.

Cacao nibs can be separated into cocoa butter and powder. Cocoa powder retains many beneficial antioxidants and is an easy way of adding cocoa into your diet without the kilojoules of chocolate.

Dutch-processed cacao powder is treated with an alkali to neutralize its acidity; it is darker and more mellow in taste.

Raw dark chocolate is made using cold-pressed raw cacao beans, that is, without the use of heat. It is high in antioxidants, and has good levels of chromium, iron and magnesium, which support healthy heart function.

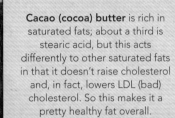

Cacao (cocoa) butter is rich in saturated fats; about a third is stearic acid, but this acts differently to other saturated fats in that it doesn't raise cholesterol and, in fact, lowers LDL (bad) cholesterol. So this makes it a pretty healthy fat overall.

CACAO

Mmmmmm, chocolate. We love it, crave it when we're feeling down, hide it for a special treat, think twice about sharing it... before we actually do. It's good to know then, that cocoa consumption has been associated with a number of health benefits.

Raw cacao powder is made by removing the cocoa butter using a process known as cold-pressing. It retains more of its nutrients than heat-processed cacao powder; it also has a stronger, slightly bitter, taste.

Cacao beans are contained inside the large cacao pod. The beans are used to make cocoa butter, cocoa powder, cocoa solids and ultimately chocolate.

banana, coffee and walnut cake with caramel sauce

185g (6 ounces) butter, softened, chopped

1 cup (245g) stevia

3 eggs

2¼ cups (335g) self-raising flour

¼ teaspoon salt

¾ teaspoon bicarbonate of soda (baking soda)

1½ teaspoons ground cinnamon

2 cups mashed ripe banana (525g)

2 teaspoons vanilla extract

¾ cup (200g) sour cream

1 cup (100g) walnut halves, roasted, chopped

¼ cup (60ml) boiling water

3 teaspoons espresso coffee granules

caramel sauce

⅔ cup (200g) rice malt syrup

125g (4 ounces) butter, softened, chopped

⅓ cup (80ml) thickened cream

1 Preheat oven to 180°C/350°F. Grease and line a deep 22cm (9-inch) round cake pan with baking paper.

2 Beat butter and stevia in a small bowl with an electric mixer until pale and fluffy. Beat in eggs, one at a time, until just combined. Transfer mixture to a large bowl. Stir sifted dry ingredients, banana, extract, sour cream, nuts and combined water and coffee into butter mixture. Spread mixture into pan.

3 Bake cake for 1¼ hours or until a skewer inserted into the centre comes out clean. Stand cake in pan for 5 minutes before turning, top-side up, onto a wire rack to cool.

4 Meanwhile, make caramel sauce; accompany cake with caramel sauce.

caramel sauce Place syrup in a small saucepan over medium heat, bring to the boil; boil for 12 minutes or until slightly dark golden in colour and the surface is covered with bubbles. Immediately add butter and cream; stir until smooth.

prep + cook time 1¾ hours serves 12
nutritional count per serving 37.2g total fat (20g saturated fat); 2235kJ (532 cal); 61.9g carbohydrate; 7g protein; 2.9g fibre

tips You will need approximately 4½ bananas to make 2 cups mashed banana. The cake can be made a day ahead; store in an airtight container at room temperature in a cool place.

olive oil marmalade cake

⅔ cup (160ml) extra virgin olive oil

1 cup (285g) cane-sugar free marmalade

3 free-range eggs

1 cup (120g) ground almonds

⅔ cup (100g) plain (all-purpose) flour

3 teaspoons baking powder

¼ cup (60ml) orange juice

orange syrup

1 medium orange (240g)

⅔ cup (160ml) orange juice

¼ cup (60ml) water

¼ cup (85g) rice malt syrup

1 cinnamon stick

3 whole cloves

1 Preheat oven to 170°C/340°F. Grease and line a deep 20cm (8-inch) round cake pan with baking paper.

2 Beat oil and marmalade in a medium bowl with an electric mixer until pale and fluffy. Add eggs one at a time, beating between each addition.

3 Sift ground almonds, flour and baking powder into a large bowl. Add almond mixture and orange juice to marmalade mixture; beat on low speed until just combined.

4 Spread mixture into pan. Bake cake for 55 minutes or until a skewer inserted into the centre comes out clean.

5 Stand cake in pan for 30 minutes before turning, top-side up, onto a wire rack.

6 Meanwhile, make orange syrup. Pierce the top of the cake randomly with a cake skewer. Slowly pour the warm syrup over the cake, allowing the syrup to be absorbed into cake. Serve cake warm or at room temperature.

orange syrup Using a vegetable peeler, thinly peel rind from orange, with as little white pith as is possible; cut rind into thin strips. Combine rind and remaining ingredients in a small saucepan; bring to the boil. Reduce heat; simmer for 15 minutes or until syrup thickens slightly. Remove from heat; cool syrup for 10 minutes. Remove cinnamon stick and cloves.

prep + cook 1¼ hours (+ standing) serves 12
nutritional count per serving 20.3g total fat (2.8g saturated fat); 1113kJ (266 cal); 15.4g carbohydrate; 5.2g protein; 2.3g fibre

chocolate hazelnut brownies

1 cup (340g) rice malt syrup

1 cup (140g) dried pitted dates, chopped coarsely

¼ teaspoon sea salt flakes

½ cup (125ml) water

½ teaspoon bicarbonate of soda (baking soda)

200g (6½ ounces) butter, chopped

3 free-range eggs

¾ cup (75g) cocoa powder

¾ cup (75g) ground hazelnuts

½ cup (75g) buckwheat flour

½ cup (120g) sour cream

½ cup (70g) whole roasted peeled hazelnuts, halved

1½ teaspoons cocoa powder, extra

1 Preheat oven to 180°C/350°F. Grease a 20cm x 30cm (8-inch x 12-inch) slice pan; line base with baking paper, extending paper 5cm (2-inches) over long sides.

2 Place syrup, dates, salt and the water in a small saucepan over low heat; simmer for 5 minutes or until dates are soft.

3 Stir soda into date mixture; transfer to a food processor, process until smooth. Return date mixture to pan; add butter, stir over medium heat until butter melts. Transfer mixture to a large bowl; cool for 5 minutes.

4 Whisk in eggs, one at a time. Stir in sifted cocoa, ground hazelnuts, flour, sour cream and chopped nuts. Spread mixture into pan; level top.

5 Bake brownie for 30 minutes or until a skewer inserted into the centre comes out with moist crumbs attached. Cool in pan before dusting with extra cocoa and cutting into squares.

prep + cook 45 minutes makes 24
nutritional count per brownie 13.3g total fat (6.2g saturated fat); 861kJ (205 cal); 19.5g carbohydrate; 2.6g protein; 1.5g fibre

tips Despite its name, buckwheat is unrelated to wheat and is known as a seed or pseduo-cereal, making it safe for those on coeliac diets. It is also high in fibre and protein.

berry and coconut chia puddings

2½ cups (625ml) coconut milk

⅓ cup (55g) white chia seeds

1 teaspoon vanilla extract

2 tablespoons honey or pure maple syrup

1 medium banana (200g), chopped coarsely

1 tablespoon finely grated orange rind

3 cups (300g) mixed berries (see tips)

1 Place coconut milk, seeds, extract and honey in a large bowl; cover, refrigerate for 1 hour or overnight until thick.

2 Blend or process coconut milk mixture with banana, rind and 2 cups of the fruit. Spoon into 6 x ¾-cup (180ml) serving glasses; refrigerate for 30 minutes or until pudding has thickened. Top with remaining fruit to serve.

prep time 15 minutes (+ refrigeration) **serves** 6
nutritional count per serving 24.6g total fat (19.2g saturated fat); 1418kJ (338 cal); 21.9g carbohydrate; 5g protein; 4.6g fibre

tips You could add some pitted cherries to the berry mix, if you like; use whatever combination of berries you like. If you have one, you can use a Thermomix or Vitamix to achieve a very smooth pudding consistency. Puddings can be made a day ahead; store, covered, in the fridge. Top with extra berries just before serving.

maple gingerbread muffins with kumara butter

1¾ cups (260g) wholemeal spelt flour

⅓ cup (40g) ground almonds

2 tablespoons ground ginger

1 teaspoon mixed spice

1½ teaspoons baking powder

¼ teaspoon bicarbonate of soda (baking soda)

3 free-range eggs

⅓ cup (80ml) olive oil

⅓ cup (80ml) pure maple syrup

¾ cup (180ml) unsweetened almond milk

1 teaspoon vanilla extract

kumara butter

400g (12½ ounces) kumara (orange sweet potato), chopped coarsely

¼ cup (50g) virgin coconut oil

1 teaspoon vanilla extract

pinch sea salt

1 Make the kumara butter.

2 Preheat oven to 160°C/325°F. Grease a 12-hole (⅓-cup/80ml) muffin pan. Cut 12 x 12cm (4¾-inch) squares of baking paper, fold into quarters, then open out again.

3 Sift flour, ground almonds, ginger, mixed spice, baking powder and soda in a large bowl. Whisk eggs, oil, syrup, milk and extract in a medium bowl until combined. Add to the dry ingredients; mix until just combined.

4 Place one square of baking paper into a pan hole; pour in ¼ cup of the batter. Repeat with the remaining baking paper squares and batter. Bake for 15 minutes or until a skewer inserted into the centre comes out clean. Serve muffins warm with kumara butter.

kumara butter Place kumara in a small saucepan, add just enough water to cover. Bring to the boil; boil for 12 minutes or until kumara is tender. Drain; return to pan, mash until smooth. Stir in oil, extract and salt. Spoon into a small bowl, cover with plastic wrap; refrigerate until butter is firm.

prep + cook time 1 hour (+ refrigeration) **makes** 12
nutritional count per serving 15.6g total fat (5.5g saturated fat); 1142kJ (272 cal); 25.4g carbohydrate; 6.8g protein; 1.4g fibre

tip Muffins are best made on the day of serving. You could also line the muffin pan with standard paper cases.

blueberry poppy seed crepes

½ cup (120g) mascarpone

125g (4 ounces) blueberries

2 teaspoons finely grated orange rind

½ cup (75g) wholemeal spelt flour

2 teaspoons poppy seeds

1 free-range egg

⅔ cup (160ml) milk

2 teaspoons rice malt syrup

1 teaspoon vanilla extract

cooking-oil spray

2 tablespoons rice malt syrup, extra

1 Place mascarpone, ⅓ cup of the blueberries and rind in a medium bowl; mash with a fork to combine.

2 Whisk flour, poppy seeds, egg, milk, syrup and extract in a small bowl.

3 Lightly spray a crêpe pan or heavy-based small frying pan with oil. Heat pan over medium heat; pour a scant ¼ cup of the batter into pan; swirl pan to coat base evenly. Cook crêpe for 2 minutes or until browned underneath. Turn, cook for a further 1 minute or until browned. Repeat with remaining crêpe batter to make a total of four crêpes.

4 Spread each crêpe with a slightly rounded tablespoon of mascarpone mixture; fold into triangles to enclose. Serve crêpes topped with remaining blueberries; drizzle with extra syrup. Serve sprinkled with thin strips of orange rind, if you like.

prep + cook time 15 minutes **makes** 4
nutritional count per crêpe 17.1g total fat (10.3g saturated fat); 1303kJ (311 cal); 32.2g carbohydrate; 7.4g protein; 0.8g fibre

earl grey and chocolate cheesecake

You need to start this recipe the day before serving. This vegan cheesecake contains no actual cheese, instead it is based on nuts, which provides a wonderful, natural richness and flavour.

8 small figs (400g), torn in half

2 teaspoons cacao powder

earl grey and chocolate filling

4 cups (600g) raw unsalted cashews

8 earl grey tea bags

¼ cup (25g) cacao powder

1 cup (230g) fresh dates, pitted

1 cup (200g) virgin coconut oil

2 teaspoons vanilla extract

cheesecake base

1 cup (170g) activated bukinis (buckwheat groats)

½ cup (80g) natural almonds

⅓ cup (35g) cacao powder

1 cup (230g) fresh dates, pitted

¼ cup (50g) virgin coconut oil

2 tablespoons warm water

1 teaspoon vanilla extract

1 Start to make the earl grey and chocolate filling by soaking the cashews and tea bags (see below).

2 Grease a 22cm (9-inch) (base measurement) springform pan; line with baking paper.

3 Make cheesecake base. Using the back of a spoon, spread the cheesecake base mixture evenly into pan; refrigerate for 15 minutes or until firm.

4 Finish preparing the filling. Spread filling over chilled base. Refrigerate for at least 4 hours or until firm. To serve, top with figs and dust with sifted cacao powder.

earl grey and chocolate filling Place nuts and tea bags in a large bowl, cover with cold water; stand for 24 hours. Drain, reserving ½ cup of the soaking liquid. Place nuts in the bowl of a food processor then empty tea leaves from tea bags over nuts. Add reserved soaking liquid, cacao, dates, oil and extract; process until mixture is as smooth as possible.

cheesecake base Process bukinis, nuts and cacao until finely ground. With the motor operating, add dates, oil, the water and extract; process until well combined and the mixture sticks together when pressed.

prep + cook time 20 minutes (+ standing & refrigeration)
serves 10
nutritional count per serving 59.2g total fat (30g saturated fat); 3457kJ (825 cal); 49.6g carbohydrate; 17g protein; 6g fibre

tips Use a hot knife to slice the cheesecake. We used activated buckinis (buckwheat) from health food stores. If you have one, you can use a Thermomix or Vitamix, which will give a very smooth filling.

little carrot cakes with date cream cheese frosting

⅓ cup (35g) sultanas

¼ cup (60ml) boiling water

2 free-range eggs

¾ cup (185g) powdered stevia

¼ cup (85g) rice malt syrup

⅔ cup (140g) virgin coconut oil, melted

2 teaspoons vanilla extract

2 cups (340g) firmly packed coarsely grated carrot

½ cup (60g) chopped pecans, roasted

1⅔ cups (250g) self-raising flour

½ teaspoon bicarbonate of soda (baking soda)

1 teaspoon ground allspice

3 teaspoons ground cinnamon

1 teaspoon ground ginger

date cream cheese frosting

125g (4 ounces) dried pitted dates, chopped finely

2 tablespoons boiling water

250g (8 ounces) cream cheese, softened

125g (4 ounces) butter, softened

1 Preheat oven to 180°C/350°F. Grease a 6-hole (¾-cup/180ml) texas muffin pan well.

2 Place sultanas in a small heatproof bowl, pour over the boiling water; stand for 10 minutes.

3 Meanwhile, whisk eggs, stevia, syrup, oil and extract in a small bowl with an electric mixer for 5 minutes. Transfer mixture to a large bowl; stir in carrot, sultanas and soaking liquid, then nuts and sifted dry ingredients. Divide mixture evenly into muffin pan holes.

4 Bake cakes for 35 minutes or until a skewer inserted into the centre of one cake comes out clean. Stand in pan for 5 minutes before turning, top-side up, onto a wire rack to cool.

5 Meanwhile, make date cream cheese frosting. Spread frosting over cake tops.

date cream cheese frosting Process dates and the boiling water until almost smooth, scraping down the side of the bowl. Add cream cheese and butter; process, scrapping down the side of the bowl, until frosting is light and fluffy.

prep + cook time 1¾ hours (+ cooling) **makes** 6
nutritional count per cake 32g total fat (21.4g saturated fat); 1882kJ (449 cal); 48.1g carbohydrate; 6.1g protein; 1.9g fibre

tips You need about 2½ medium carrots to make 2 cups grated carrot. You could also cook the cake recipe as a slice using a 20cm x 30cm x 3cm (8-inch x 12-inch x 1¼-inch) slice pan. Line the base with baking paper, extending paper 5cm (2-inches) over the long sides; bake for 25 minutes.

watermelon and lemon tea granita

You need to make this recipe the day before serving.

1 herbal lemon tea bag

1 cup (250ml) boiling water

1 tablespoon powdered stevia or norbu
(monk fruit sugar)

500g (1 pound) seedless watermelon, chopped

1½ tablespoons lemon juice

600g (1¼ pounds) seedless watermelon, extra,
sliced thinly

fennel salt

1 tablespoon sea salt flakes

1 teaspoon fennel seeds

1 teaspoon finely grated lemon rind

1 Steep the tea bag in the boiling water for 10 minutes; discard tea bag. Stir stevia into tea until dissolved.

2 Blend or process the watermelon until smooth. Stir in tea and lemon juice. Pour into a 2.5-litre (10 cup) shallow dish.

3 Freeze granita for 1 hour. Using a fork, break up any ice crystals. Freeze for a further 6 hours, scraping with a fork every hour or until frozen.

4 Make fennel salt.

5 Divide extra watermelon among serving glasses, top with granita and sprinkle with fennel salt.

fennel salt Using a pestle and mortar, crush salt, seeds and rind. (Alternatively, place in a small bowl and crush with the back of a wooden spoon.)

prep time 20 minutes (+ freezing) **serves** 6
nutritional count per serving 0.3g total fat (0g saturated fat); 134kJ (32 cal); 6.3g carbohydrate; 0.5g protein; 0.7g fibre

tips Stevia and norbu are both natural sweeteners available from major supermarkets: for information, see pages 230-231. Top with thin strips of lemon or orange rind, if you like.

flourless almond, plum and orange blossom loaf

2 medium green apples (300g), grated coarsely

2 free-range eggs, beaten lightly

¼ cup (60ml) unsweetened almond milk

2 tablespoons honey or pure maple syrup

2 teaspoons vanilla extract

1 teaspoon orange blossom water

2 cups (240g) ground almonds

2 teaspoons gluten-free baking powder

5 small plums (375g), halved

2 teaspoons honey or pure maple syrup, extra

2 tablespoons flaked coconut, toasted

1 Preheat oven to 160°C/325°F. Lightly grease a 10.5cm x 21cm x 6cm (4-inch x 8½-inch x 2½-inch) (base measurement) loaf pan; line base and long sides with baking paper.

2 Combine apple, egg, milk, honey, extract and orange blossom water in a large bowl. Add ground almonds and baking powder; stir until just combined.

3 Spread mixture into pan, level top; top with plums, cut-side up, pressing them slightly into the batter. Drizzle with extra honey. Bake for 1¾ hours or until a skewer inserted into the centre comes out clean. Sprinkle with coconut and serve warm.

prep + cook time 1½ hours **serves** 6

nutritional count per serving 26.3g total fat (3.1g saturated fat); 1535kJ (366 cal); 19.7g carbohydrate; 11.2g protein; 5.7g fibre

tips You can also make this loaf with other stone fruit such as small peaches or apricots. You may need to cover the loaf loosely with baking paper during the last 10 minutes of baking to prevent overbrowning.

For paleo and dairy-free diets, serve with coconut yoghurt.

strawberry halva mousse

2 cups (500ml) coconut cream (see tips)

250g (8 ounces) strawberries

¼ cup (90g) honey

2 teaspoons vanilla extract

1 cup (280g) greek-style yoghurt

¾ cup (210g) unhulled tahini (sesame seed paste)

250g (8 ounces) strawberries, extra, sliced

¼ cup (35g) pistachios, chopped

1 tablespoon sesame seeds, toasted

⅓ cup (65g) pomegranate seeds

1 Pour coconut cream into a medium metal bowl; place in the freezer for 30 minutes or until chilled.

2 Blend or process strawberries, 1 tablespoon of the honey and half the extract until smooth.

3 Whisk coconut cream, yoghurt, tahini and remaining honey and extract until thickened slightly, then swirl through the strawberry mixture.

4 Divide mixture among 6 x 1-cup (250ml) serving glasses; cover, refrigerate for 2 hours or until firm.

5 Serve topped with sliced strawberries, pistachios, sesame and pomegranate seeds.

prep time 30 minutes (+ freezing & refrigeration) **serves** 6
nutritional count per serving 43g total fat (19.6g saturated fat); 2482kJ (593 cal); 36.5g carbohydrate; 15.7g protein; 2.1g fibre

tips Use a brand of coconut cream that states it is 100% natural on the label. Coconut cream that has 'emulsifying agents' added (it will state this on the label) may cause the mousse to separate into creamy and watery layers. You can make the mousse a day ahead; store, covered, in the fridge.
For vegan diets, substitute coconut milk yoghurt for the greek-style yoghurt.

cacao and hazelnut cookies

½ cup (80g) firmly packed fresh dates, pitted

2 cups (200g) ground hazelnuts

1½ cups (225g) wholemeal spelt flour

¼ cup (50g) chia seeds

1 teaspoon ground cinnamon

pinch sea salt flakes

¼ cup (50g) virgin coconut oil, at room temperature

½ cup (170g) rice malt syrup

1 free-range egg

2 teaspoons vanilla extract

½ cup (50g) cacao nibs

1 Preheat oven to 160°C/325°F. Line two oven trays with baking paper.

2 Place dates in a small heatproof bowl, cover with boiling water; stand for 5 minutes. Drain.

3 Process dates, ground hazelnuts, flour, seeds, cinnamon, salt, oil, syrup, egg and extract until well combined. Stir in cacao nibs.

4 Using damp hands, roll 2-tablespoonfuls of mixture into a ball, place on tray; flatten with the palm of your hand into a 6cm (2½-inch) round. Using the back of a damp fork, mark each cookie. Bake for 15 minutes or until a cookie can gently be pushed without breaking. Cool cookies on trays.

prep + cook time 30 minutes **makes** 16
nutritional count per cookie 16.1g total fat (4g saturated fat); 1105kJ (264 cal); 22.7g carbohydrate; 5.9g protein; 2.7g fibre

tip Cacao nibs are created in the early stages of chocolate production; cocoa beans are dried then roasted, after which they are crushed into what is termed 'nibs'. The nibs are then ground to separate the cocoa butter and cocoa solids. Nibs are both textural and chocolatey with no sweetness. They can be found at health food stores and specialist food stores.

Monk fruit is a subtropical melon that has been grown for hundreds of years in South-East Asia. The fruit contains a group of sweet tasting antioxidant compounds. A little like stevia, these compounds deliver sweetness without the sugar and kilojoules. Monk fruit sugar has 96% fewer kilojoules than sugar, and will not affect blood glucose or insulin levels.

Honey is one of the most natural sweeteners we can use. Local flora makes an impact on the flavour of the honey. Pure floral honeys have a low GI, but cheaper, blended honeys tend to be high. For a low GI honey look for Yellow Box, Stringy Bark, Red Gum, Iron Bark, Yapunya, Eucalypt or those labelled as pure floral honey.

Fresh honeycomb is the structure made of beeswax that houses the honey; it is an edible chewy comb, saturated with honey.

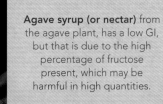

Agave syrup (or nectar) from the agave plant, has a low GI, but that is due to the high percentage of fructose present, which may be harmful in high quantities.

Barley malt syrup, made from sprouted barley, isn't as sweet as sugar or honey. It is produced similarly to brown rice syrup.

Brown rice syrup is made by cooking brown rice flour with enzymes to break down its starch into sugars from which the water is removed.

SUGAR-FREE

The popularity of cutting sugar from our diet comes with much confusion. Sure, cutting out processed and packaged foods, which are full of added sugar, makes sense, but we certainly shouldn't be cutting out fruits and vegetables, which are also full of beneficial antioxidants, vitamins, minerals and fibre.

Pure maple syrup is the concentrated sap of the maple tree, whereas maple-flavoured syrups are usually just processed glucose syrup with added flavourings. Real maple syrup is much tastier and contains significant amounts of nutrients and antioxidant compounds. It has a low GI, making it a good choice for blood glucose control.

Stevia comes from a plant, so is promoted as a natural sweetener, however, once processed, the end product becomes highly refined. It has a minimal effect on blood glucose levels and has no kilojoules, so it can be a useful way to reduce sugar intakes.

cinnamon and fig baked apples

¼ cup (35g) roasted hazelnuts, peeled

3 dried figs

6 pitted prunes

½ teaspoon ground cinnamon

1 teaspoon vanilla extract

6 large red apples (1.2kg), cored (see tip)

ricotta cream

1 cup (240g) fresh firm ricotta

½ cup (125ml) milk

1 teaspoon vanilla extract

½ teaspoon finely grated mandarin rind

maple sauce

2 large mandarins (500g)

¼ cup (60ml) maple syrup

30g (1 ounce) cold butter, chopped finely

1 Preheat oven to 160°C/325°F. Line oven tray with baking paper.

2 Process hazelnuts, figs, prunes, cinnamon and extract until coarsely chopped.

3 Using a small, sharp knife, score around the centre of each apple. Press hazelnut mixture into the cavities of each apple; place apples upright on tray. Bake for 30 minutes or until apples are tender.

4 Meanwhile, make ricotta cream. Make maple sauce.

5 Serve apples with ricotta cream and maple sauce.

ricotta cream Process ricotta, milk and extract until smooth; stir in rind.

maple sauce Squeeze juice from mandarins; you will need ⅔ cup. Place juice and maple syrup in a small saucepan over medium heat; simmer until reduced by half and mixture is syrupy. Remove pan from heat; whisk in butter a few pieces at a time, until melted and combined.

prep + cook time 40 minutes **serves** 6

nutritional count per serving 13.2g total fat (6.4g saturated fat); 1683kJ (402 cal); 61g carbohydrate; 7.9g protein; 5.6g fibre

tip We used royal gala apples.

glossary

activated buckinis made with buckwheat, which, despite its name, is not actually a wheat, but is a fruit belonging to the same family as strawberries. It's gluten free, high in protein and essential amino acids, and is a rich source of minerals and B vitamins.

allspice also known as pimento or jamaican pepper; so-named because it tastes like a combination of nutmeg, cumin, clove and cinnamon. Available whole or ground.

almonds flat, pointy-tipped creamy white kernel with a brown skin.

blanched brown skins removed.

flaked paper-thin slices.

baking paper also called parchment paper or baking parchment – is a silicone-coated paper that is primarily used for lining baking pans and oven trays so cooked food doesn't stick, making removal easy.

barley a nutritious grain used in soups and stews. Hulled barley, the least processed, is high in fibre. Pearl barley has had the husk removed then been steamed and polished so that only the 'pearl' of the original grain remains, much the same as white rice.

bay leaves aromatic leaves from the bay tree available fresh or dried; adds a strong, slightly peppery flavour.

beans

borlotti also called roman beans or pink beans, can be eaten fresh or dried. Interchangeable with pinto beans due to their similarity in appearance – pale pink or beige with dark red streaks.

broad (fava) also called windsor and horse beans; available dried, fresh, canned and frozen. Fresh should be peeled twice (discarding the outer long green pod and the beige-green tough inner shell); frozen beans have had their pods removed but the beige shell still needs removal.

cannellini a small white bean similar in appearance and flavour to other white beans (great northern, navy or haricot), all of which can be substituted for the other. Available dried or canned.

kidney medium-sized red bean, slightly floury in texture, yet sweet in flavour.

white a generic term we use for canned or cannellini, haricot, navy or great northern beans belonging to the same family; all can be used.

bee pollen is collected and sold as a health-food product with claims of being 'nature's perfect food', However, there have been documented cases of severe anaphylactic reactions to bee pollen. Pregnant and breast-feeding mothers should avoid bee pollen.

beetroot (beets) also known as red beets; firm, round root vegetable.

bicarbonate of soda (baking soda) a raising agent.

breadcrumbs

panko (japanese) are available in two kinds: larger pieces and fine crumbs; has a lighter texture than Western-style ones. Available from Asian food stores and most supermarkets.

stale made by grating, blending or processing 1- or 2-day-old bread.

broccolini a cross between broccoli and chinese kale; it has long asparagus-like stems with a long loose floret, both are completely edible. Resembles broccoli but is milder and sweeter in taste.

buk choy also known as bok choy, pak choi, chinese white cabbage or chinese chard; has a fresh, mild mustard taste. Use both stems and leaves. Baby buk choy is milder and more tender than buk choy.

butter use salted or unsalted (sweet) butter; 125g is equal to one stick of butter (4 ounces).

buttermilk originally the term given to the slightly sour liquid left after butter was churned from cream, today it is made from no-fat or low-fat milk to which specific bacterial cultures have been added. Despite its name, it is actually low in fat.

capers grey-green buds of a warm climate shrub (usually Mediterranean); sold dried and salted or pickled in a vinegar brine. Rinse before using.

capsicum (bell pepper) also called pepper. Comes in many colours: red, green, yellow, orange and purplish-black. Be sure to discard seeds and membranes before use.

cardamom a spice native to India and used extensively in its cuisine; can be purchased in pod, seed or ground form. Has a distinctive aromatic, sweetly rich flavour.

celeriac (celery root) tuberous root with knobbly brown skin, white flesh and a celery-like flavour. Keep peeled celeriac in acidulated water to stop it discolouring. It can be grated and eaten raw in salads; used in stews; mashed like potatoes; or sliced and deep-fried as chips.

cheese

fetta Greek in origin; a crumbly textured goat- or sheep-milk cheese having a sharp, salty taste. Ripened and stored in salted whey.

fetta, persian a soft, creamy fetta marinated in a blend of olive oil, garlic, herbs and spices. It is available from most larger supermarkets.

goat's made from goat's milk, has an earthy, strong taste; available in both soft and firm textures, in various shapes and sizes, and sometimes rolled in ash or herbs.

haloumi a firm, cream-coloured sheep-milk cheese matured in brine; haloumi can be grilled or fried, briefly, without breaking down. Should be eaten while still warm as it becomes tough and rubbery on cooling.

parmesan also called parmigiano; is a hard, grainy cow-milk cheese originating in Italy. Reggiano is the best variety.

pecorino the Italian generic name for cheeses made from sheep milk; hard, white to pale-yellow cheeses. If you can't find it, use parmesan.

ricotta a soft, sweet, moist, white cow-milk cheese with a low fat content and a slightly grainy texture. The name roughly translates as 'cooked again' and refers to ricotta's manufacture from a whey that is itself a by-product of other cheese making.

chickpeas (garbanzo beans) an irregularly round, sandy-coloured legume. Has a firm texture even after cooking, a floury mouth-feel and robust nutty flavour; available canned or dried (reconstitute for several hours in cold water before use).

chilli available in many different types and sizes. Use rubber gloves when seeding and chopping fresh chillies as they can burn your skin. Removing seeds and membranes lessens the heat level.

cayenne pepper a long, thin-fleshed, extremely hot red chilli usually sold dried and ground.

green any unripened chilli; also some particular varieties that are ripe when green, such as jalapeño, habanero, poblano or serrano.

long available both fresh and dried; a generic term used for any moderately hot, thin, long (6-8cm/2¼-3¼ inch) chilli.

red thai also known as 'scuds'; small, very hot and bright red; can be substituted with fresh serrano or habanero chillies.

chinese cooking wine (shao hsing) also known as chinese rice wine; made from fermented rice, wheat, sugar and salt with a 13.5% alcohol content. Inexpensive and found in Asian food shops; if you can't find it, replace with mirin or sherry.

chinese five-spice powder a fragrant mixture of ground cinnamon, cloves, star anise, sichuan pepper and fennel seeds.

choy sum also known as pakaukeo or flowering cabbage, a member of the buk choy family; easy to identify with its long stems, light green leaves and yellow flowers. Stems and leaves are edible.

cinnamon available in sticks (quills) and ground into powder; used as a sweet, fragrant flavouring in sweet and savoury foods.

cocoa powder also known as cocoa; dried, unsweetened, roasted and ground cocoa beans (cacao seeds).

dutch-processed is treated with an alkali to neutralise its acids. It has a reddish-brown colour, a mild flavour and easily dissolves in liquids.

coconut

flaked dried flaked coconut flesh.

milk not the liquid found inside the fruit (coconut water), but the diluted liquid from the second pressing of the white flesh of a mature coconut (the first pressing produces coconut cream).

coriander (cilantro) also known as pak chee or chinese parsley; a bright-green leafy herb with a pungent flavour. Both the stems and roots of coriander are also used in cooking; wash well before using. Also available ground or as seeds; these should not be substituted for fresh coriander as the tastes are completely different.

couscous a fine, grain-like cereal product made from semolina; it swells to three or four times its original size when liquid is added.

cumin also known as zeera or comino; has a spicy, nutty flavour.

dukkah an Egyptian specialty spice mixture made up of roasted nuts, seeds and an array of aromatic spices.

edamame (shelled soy beans) available frozen from Asian food stores and some supermarkets.

eggplant also known as aubergine. Ranging in size from tiny to very large and in colour from pale green to deep purple.

fennel also known as finocchio or anise; a white to very pale green-white, firm, crisp, roundish vegetable about 8-12cm in diameter. The bulb has a slightly sweet, anise flavour but the leaves have a much stronger taste. Also the name given to dried seeds having a licorice flavour.

fish sauce called naam pla (Thai) and nuoc naam (Vietnamese); the two are almost identical. Made from pulverised salted fermented fish (often anchovies); has a pungent smell and strong taste. Available in varying degrees of intensity, so use according to your taste.

flour

chickpea (besan) made from ground chickpeas so is gluten-free and high in protein. Used in Indian cooking.

plain (all-purpose) an all-purpose wheat flour.

self-raising plain flour sifted with baking powder in the proportion of 1 cup flour to 2 teaspoons baking powder.

wholemeal also known as wholewheat flour; milled with the wheat germ so is higher in fibre and more nutritional than plain flour.

gai lan also known as chinese broccoli, gai larn, kanah, gai lum and chinese kale; appreciated more for its stems than its coarse leaves.

germinating sprouts *A word of warning if you want to germinate sprouts, or when eating sprouts:* the warm moist conditions necessary are also perfect for the growth of pathogenic bacteria such as E. Coli and listeria, which can cause severe illness. For this reason, those most at risk – pregnant women, infants and young children, those with compromised immune systems, and the elderly – should avoid raw sprouts. However, everyone can enjoy cooked sprouts, as heating thoroughly kills these bacteria making them safe to eat.

Getting started: clean beans/seeds are essential; be sure to buy organic sprouting beans from a reputable store. Wash the beans thoroughly and remove any small twigs, stones or broken or split beans. Place beans in a clean large glass jar (the beans will expand as they soak and increase in size as they sprout) and fill with water. Cover with muslin and secure with a rubber band; soak the beans for 8 to 12 hours at room temperature (usually, the larger the bean, the longer it needs to be soaked).

After the initial soaking: drain the water through the muslin, then rinse and drain again. Place the jar, still covered with the muslin, upside-down on an angle, on a dish rack or wire rack so the remaining moisture drains through the muslin. Keep the jar away from the sunlight, and make sure the air can circulate around the opening. Rinse and drain the beans with fresh water at least twice a day (or up to four times a day if the beans are starting to dry out completely). Keep doing this until the sprouts grow to the length you want, usually in about 3-5 days.

ginger, pickled pink or red in colour, paper-thin shavings of ginger pickled in a mixture of vinegar, sugar and natural colouring. Available from Asian food shops.

kaffir lime leaves also known as bai magrood. Aromatic leaves of a citrus tree; two glossy dark green leaves joined end to end, forming a rounded hourglass shape. A strip of fresh lime peel may be substituted for each kaffir lime leaf.

kecap manis a thick soy sauce with added sugar and spices. The sweetness is derived from the addition of molasses or palm sugar.

kumara (orange sweet potato) the Polynesian name of an orange-fleshed sweet potato often confused with yam.

labne is a soft cheese made by salting plain (natural) yoghurt and draining it of whey for up to 2 days until it becomes thick enough to roll into small balls, which may be sprinkled with or rolled in chopped herbs or spices.

leeks a member of the onion family, the leek resembles a green onion but is much larger and more subtle in flavour. Tender baby or pencil leeks can be eaten whole with minimal cooking but adult leeks are usually trimmed of most of the green tops then chopped or sliced.

lentils (red, brown, yellow) dried pulses often identified by and named after their colour; also known as dhal.

french-style green are a local cousin to the famous French lentils du puy; green-blue, tiny lentils with a nutty, earthy flavour and a hardy nature that allows them to be rapidly cooked without disintegrating.

maple syrup, pure distilled from the sap of sugar maple trees found only in Canada and the USA. Maple-flavoured syrup or pancake syrup is not an adequate substitute for the real thing.

mushrooms

enoki clumps of long, spaghetti-like stems with tiny, snowy white caps.

flat large, flat mushrooms with a rich earthy flavour. They are sometimes misnamed field mushrooms, which are wild mushrooms.

oyster also known as abalone; grey-white mushroom shaped like a fan. Prized for their smooth texture and subtle, oyster-like flavour.

shiitake when fresh are also called chinese black, forest or golden oak mushrooms; although cultivated, they are large and meaty and have the earthiness and taste of wild mushrooms. When dried, they are called donko or dried chinese mushrooms; rehydrate before use.

swiss brown also known as cremini or roman mushrooms, are light brown mushrooms having a full-bodied flavour.

muslin inexpensive, undyed, finely woven cotton fabric called for in cooking to strain stocks and sauces; if unavailable, use disposable coffee filter papers.

mustard seeds are available in black, brown or yellow varieties. They are available from major supermarkets and health-food shops.

noodles, soba thin, pale-brown noodle originally from Japan; made from buckwheat and varying proportions of wheat flour.

onions

green (scallions) also known as, incorrectly, shallot; an immature onion picked before the bulb has formed. Has a long, bright-green edible stalk.

red also known as spanish, red spanish or bermuda onion; a sweet-flavoured, large, purple-red onion.

shallots also called french shallots, golden shallots or eschalots; small, brown-skinned, elongated members of the onion family.

pepitas (pumpkin seeds) are the pale green kernels of dried pumpkin seeds; they can be bought plain or salted.

pine nuts not a nut but a small, cream-coloured kernel from pine cones. They are best roasted before use to bring out the flavour.

pomegranate dark-red, leathery-skinned fresh fruit about the size of an orange filled with hundreds of seeds, each wrapped in an edible lucent-crimson pulp having a unique tangy sweet-sour flavour.

pomegranate molasses not to be confused with pomegranate syrup or grenadine; pomegranate molasses is thicker, browner and more concentrated in flavour – tart, sharp, slightly sweet and fruity. Available from Middle Eastern food stores or specialty food shops.

quinoa pronounced keen-wa; is a gluten-free grain. It has a delicate, slightly nutty taste and chewy texture.

radicchio a red-leafed Italian chicory with a refreshing bitter taste that's eaten raw or grilled. Comes in varieties named after their places of origin, such as round-headed verona or long-headed treviso.

rice

basmati a white, fragrant long-grained rice. Wash several times before cooking.

jasmine fragrant long-grained rice; white rice can be substituted, but will not taste the same.

roasting/toasting nuts and seeds

desiccated coconut, pine nuts and sesame seeds roast more evenly if stirred over low heat in a heavy-based frying pan; their natural oils will help turn them golden brown. Remove from pan immediately.

nuts and dried coconut can be roasted in the oven to release their aromatic essential oils. Spread them evenly onto an oven tray then roast at 180°C/350°F for about 5 minutes.

saffron available ground or in strands; imparts a yellow-orange colour to food once infused. The quality can vary greatly; the best is the most expensive spice in the world.

silver beet also known as swiss chard; mistakenly called spinach.

snow peas also called mange tout (eat all). Snow pea tendrils, the growing shoots of the plant, are also available at greengrocers.

sprouts are the tender new growths of snow peas.

soy sauce made from fermented soy beans. Several variations are available in most supermarkets and Asian food stores. We use japanese soy sauce unless otherwise indicated.

spinach also known as english spinach and, incorrectly, silver beet. Baby spinach leaves are best eaten raw in salads; the larger leaves should be added last to soups, stews and stir-fries, and should be cooked until barely wilted.

sugar

brown very soft, finely granulated sugar retaining molasses for its characteristic colour and flavour.

caster (superfine) finely granulated table sugar.

palm also called nam tan pip, jaggery, jawa or gula melaka; made from the sap of the sugar palm tree. Light brown to black in colour and usually sold in rock-hard cakes; use brown sugar if unavailable.

sumac a purple-red, astringent spice ground from berries growing on shrubs that flourish wild around the Mediterranean; adds a tart, lemony flavour to food. Available from spice shops and major supermarkets.

tahini a rich, sesame-seed paste, used in most Middle-Eastern cuisines, especially Lebanese, in dips and sauces.

tamarind the tamarind tree produces clusters of hairy brown pods, each of which is filled with seeds and a viscous pulp, that are dried and pressed into the blocks of tamarind found in Asian food shops. Gives a sweet-sour, slightly astringent taste to marinades, sauces and dressings.

turmeric also called kamin; is a rhizome related to galangal and ginger. Must be grated or pounded to release its acrid aroma and pungent flavour. Known for the golden colour it imparts, fresh turmeric can be substituted with the more commonly found dried powder.

vinegar

balsamic originally from Modena, Italy, there are now many balsamic vinegars on the market ranging in pungency and quality depending on how, and for how long, they have been aged. Quality can be determined up to a point by price; use the most expensive sparingly.

white balsamic is a clear and lighter version of balsamic vinegar; it has a fresh, sweet, clean taste.

watercress one of the cress family, a large group of peppery greens. Highly perishable, so must be used as soon as possible after purchase. It has an exceptionally high vitamin K content, which is terrific for eye health, and is an excellent source of calcium.

yeast (dried and fresh), a raising agent used in dough making. Granular (7g sachets) and fresh compressed (20g blocks) yeast can almost always be substituted for the other.

conversion chart

measures

One Australian metric measuring cup holds approximately 250ml; one Australian metric tablespoon holds 20ml; one Australian metric teaspoon holds 5ml. The difference between one country's measuring cups and another's is within a two- or three-teaspoon variance, and will not affect your cooking results. North America, New Zealand and the United Kingdom use a 15ml tablespoon.

All cup and spoon measurements are level. The most accurate way of measuring dry ingredients is to weigh them. When measuring liquids, use a clear glass or plastic jug with the metric markings.

The imperial measurements used in these recipes are approximate only. Measurements for cake pans are approximate only. Using same-shaped cake pans of a similar size should not affect the outcome of your baking. We measure the inside top of the cake pan to determine sizes.

We use large eggs with an average weight of 60g.

dry measures

metric	imperial
15g	½oz
30g	1oz
60g	2oz
90g	3oz
125g	4oz (¼lb)
155g	5oz
185g	6oz
220g	7oz
250g	8oz (½lb)
280g	9oz
315g	10oz
345g	11oz
375g	12oz (¾lb)
410g	13oz
440g	14oz
470g	15oz
500g	16oz (1lb)
750g	24oz (1½lb)
1kg	32oz (2lb)

liquid measures

metric	imperial
30ml	1 fluid oz
60ml	2 fluid oz
100ml	3 fluid oz
125ml	4 fluid oz
150ml	5 fluid oz
190ml	6 fluid oz
250ml	8 fluid oz
300ml	10 fluid oz
500ml	16 fluid oz
600ml	20 fluid oz
1000ml (1 litre)	1¾ pints

length measures

metric	imperial
3mm	⅛in
6mm	¼in
1cm	½in
2cm	¾in
2.5cm	1in
5cm	2in
6cm	2½in
8cm	3in
10cm	4in
13cm	5in
15cm	6in
18cm	7in
20cm	8in
22cm	9in
25cm	10in
28cm	11in
30cm	12in (1ft)

oven temperatures

The oven temperatures in this book are for conventional ovens; if you have a fan-forced oven, decrease the temperature by 10-20 degrees.

	°C (CELSIUS)	°F (FAHRENHEIT)
Very slow	120	250
Slow	150	300
Moderately slow	160	325
Moderate	180	350
Moderately hot	200	400
Hot	220	425
Very hot	240	475

index